THE SOVIET DEPORTATION
OF NATIONALITIES

THE SOVIET DEPORTATION OF NATIONALITIES

BY

R. CONQUEST

LATELY RESEARCH FELLOW OF THE LONDON SCHOOL
OF ECONOMICS AND POLITICAL SCIENCE

LONDON
MACMILLAN & CO LTD
NEW YORK · ST MARTIN'S PRESS
1960

MACMILLAN AND COMPANY LIMITED
London Bombay Calcutta Madras Melbourne

THE MACMILLAN COMPANY OF CANADA LIMITED
Toronto

ST MARTIN'S PRESS INC
New York

PRINTED IN GREAT BRITAIN

For My Father

'The official programme of the Party is less important than what it actually does.'

(Letter from Engels to Bebel, March 1875. Quoted in Appendix I, *Critique of the Gotha Programme*, London, 1933.)

CONTENTS

Note: Chapters 8 and 9 are based in part on material used at a seminar held at the London School of Economics and Political Science in 1957.

LIST OF MAPS

INTRODUCTION

———◦◦◦———

THIS book is concerned with one of the most significant, and most neglected, episodes in modern history: the fate of seven minority nations of the U.S.S.R. who were deported entire from their native countries during the war and five of whom were rehabilitated in 1957.

The treatment of these peoples by successive governments of the Soviet Union is a test case of the whole nature of Communist national policy and of much more. I have dealt not only with the events themselves but with the political and ideological context in which they could occur. This book does not claim to be definitive. This is partly because I have, except in Chapter 7, largely confined myself to Soviet sources, mainly with the purpose of putting the facts beyond controversy. But it will be obvious that there is naturally a good deal more that has emerged from refugees and other unofficial sources, and of which I have only given short accounts.

My main purpose has been to tell the story of the deportations and the events which followed as objectively and straightforwardly as possible, and to go into the reasons for them. But I have also tried to assemble all the documentary evidence that can be thought of as essential, and much that is simply illustrative as well. The events, and the official explanations of them are so extraordinary that it seems to the writer that the story becomes more rather than less dramatic by being presented so largely through the hard officialese of decrees and articles.

On the pre-deportation history of the peoples, early Soviet authorities are reasonably accurate as to facts, though their general interpretations may be controversial, to say the least. It seems particularly appropriate to quote, where possible, from the historical, political and ethnographical assessments given in the first edition of the *Large Soviet Encyclopaedia*, in preference to other accounts, when dealing with the official views held about these nations in the early Soviet period. For not only do they often summarize conveniently and officially the ideas generally expressed at the time, but they can be compared perfectly fairly, and with extraordinary results, with their equivalents in the second edition of the same work.

For a description of the results of Soviet national policy over the whole of the U.S.S.R., the reader is referred to Mr. Walter Kolarz's two books *Russia and Her Colonies* and *Peoples of the Soviet Far East*. Colonel Hostler's *Turkism and the Soviets* is a very thorough study of the position of the Turkic minorities in the U.S.S.R., three of which were among the deported nations.

．　．　．　．　．

On the southern borderlands of Russia proper lie a number of mainly Asian peoples, most of whom formerly occupied much larger territories. The ones who suffered deportation can be considered in three groups as far as the history of their annexation to Moscow was concerned.

First there are the Volga Germans, who were brought into the territory as favoured immigrants by the Russian authorities themselves.

Second are the Kalmyks, inhabiting the steppe south-west of Astrakhan, who came fairly completely under Russian influence as early as the end of the seventeenth century.

And third, the Mohammedan nations of the Crimea and the North Caucasus, territories which the Russians only invaded at the end of the eighteenth century, and did not finally subdue until the latter half of the nineteenth. The Crimea was annexed only in 1783, at the time of the British annexation of Oudh, and by similar methods. The North Caucasian annexations were only completed in the 1860's at the time of the British annexations in Africa. In fact, these territories are not old Russian lands, or even old dependencies, but were annexed as part of the great wave of European imperialist expansion.

A comparison may indeed be made between the present situation of those parts of Asia similarly and simultaneously brought under the rule of Britain and Russia. The present map shows, instead of a vast stretch of dependent territory from the Persian Gulf to the China Sea, a few islands and strips of coast still coming under London's control. The area under Moscow's control remains the same as in Tsarist times. The Soviet argument, indeed, is that the Caucasian and other territories involved enjoy complete autonomy and are voluntarily united with Russia. This thesis is examined in Chapter 9.

These nations were deported in 1941 (the Volga Germans) and in 1943–4. The Volga Germans were in a way a special case. The other six were a majority of the small peoples reached, or nearly reached, by the German invasion. This fact lends force to Kolarz's statement, in his *Russia and Her Colonies*, that:

> The liquidation of the republics was a warning to all other non-Russian peoples, many of whom might have found themselves in the same position had their loyalty to Russia been put to the same test as that of the Volga Germans, Crimean Tatars, and Kalmyks. Had the U.S.S.R. been invaded by Japan, the Autonomous Republics of the Yakuts and Buryato-Mongols might have suffered the fate of the Crimean and Kalmyk Republics; had it been Turkey, a similar doom might have been the lot of the Azerbaidzhani Turks.

The two main Asian minority groups of the communist empires were involved: the Muslim Turki and the Buddhist Mongol. *All* the Turkic and Mongol nations reached by the Germans were deported — in addition to others such as the Chechens who belonged to neither group.

The story of these unfortunate people illustrates not only the Soviet national policy but a good deal else in Soviet practices. It shows events taking place in the Soviet Union of which information can be prevented, or largely prevented, from reaching the outside world. It shows how in the Soviet Union itself facts of considerable importance can simply never be published anywhere if official policy so decides. It shows the size of deportation operations which (now admittedly) have been undertaken by the Soviet authorities. It casts a considerable light on police methods in general in the U.S.S.R. It gives a clear example of how history can be rewritten. And the fact that certain Soviet claims, about the prosperity and general contentment of sections of the population, are shown to have been entirely false is relevant to the validity of Soviet claims in general. On a minor point, in this connection, the validity of the quasi-unanimous votes cast in Soviet elections may be checked by the fact that the deported nations joined in these demonstrations in the same proportion as their fellows. And, to conclude, it also seems not unreasonable to judge the adequacy of official Soviet literary products by the fact that these peoples had been equipped with 'literatures' of adulation for Stalin and other party-line matter.

There is nothing in the story which compares with the spectacular horrors of the Nazi gas chambers. (It is a sad comment on our times that not to have behaved as badly as the Nazis may be regarded as a sign of virtue.) But there are other ways of destroying a nation. To remove it, in circumstances of 'misery and suffering' from its homeland, and scatter it widely over an alien territory, with a minimum of economic resources, deprived of civil rights, of cultural opportunities and of education in its own tongue is, even leaving aside the high incidence of actual deaths, a sign that the aim can hardly be other than the extinction of the nation, as a nation. When rather similar measures were practised in the case of the Hereros in South-West Africa, before the first world war, what was then called the conscience of the civilized world was appalled, and the reversal of the policy was secured. The Soviet Government, under similar pressures to those applied to the Government of Imperial Germany, eventually made partial restitution. The change of policy is welcome, but it does not erase the original intent or actions.

The aim of this book is both to present the documentation, which does not seem to have been so assembled before, in a form convenient for students of the matter, and at the same time to give, as a context, enough of the background to make it easy for the general reader to follow the story. The amount of quotation and reference might in an ordinary case make it indigestible from the latter's point of view. But there are certain problems, like the Dead Sea Scrolls, or the decipherment of Minoan B Script by the late Mr. Ventris, in which it is evident that the sheer intrinsic interest of the deductions can lead the reader through a good deal of this type of thing, without exhaustion. And I believe that the theme of this book and its rather similar probing of obscure secrets may possibly do the same.

Chapter 1

THE RUSSIANS ARRIVE

W e usually think of the Middle East as a Moham-
medan-Asian territory bounded on the north by the
Soviet frontier and the Black and Caspian Seas. But
the regions to the north of this boundary are as much Asian —
and largely Mohammedan — as those to the south.

Parenthetically, it may be noted that while it is now com-
monest in Britain and elsewhere to regard the watershed of the
Caucasus as marking the frontier of Europe, the Russian
preference is still to regard the line of the Kuma-Manych
Depression as the physical boundary between the continents.

Russia's expansion into the whole area is very recent. The
first Russian kingdom arose in what is now the Ukraine, but
was destroyed in the middle ages by the Mongols. The new
Russia which came into being round Moscow expanded in
three directions: northwards, where it absorbed and largely
Russianized the Finnish tribes inhabiting what is now North
Russia; eastwards through the comparatively empty stretches
of Siberia, reaching the Pacific in the seventeenth century; and,
much more slowly, southwards into the area where great
Mohammedan and Buddhist states were already established.
Russia did not even obtain a final foothold on the Sea of
Azov until 1739, and not on the Black Sea proper until 1774.
What is now the Ukraine was in the possession of the Crimean
Tatars, or an empty border space in which bands of Russians
to whom the authoritarian regime was intolerable set up their
own quasi-independent Cossack commonwealths. The first
Russian expansion consisted of the conquest of the Moham-

medan Khanates which stretched right up to the Volga and the Urals. Kazan fell in 1552 and Astrakhan in 1556. The collapse of the Astrakhan Khanate left what we now call a power vacuum in the area between that city and the Northern Caucasus. Over this area the Khans of the Crimea, the Persians, and the Khans of Astrakhan had long maintained rival claims to suzerainty. Russia now stood as the successor state to Astrakhan.

Two local political formations dominated the North-east Caucasus. One was a sort of federation — 'the Princes of Kabarda'—to the west. The other, the principality of Tarki, headed by its Shavkal, lay in the north of Daghestan. The Kabardines had relied on Astrakhan for support against the Crimea, and when Russia conquered Astrakhan they almost immediately formed a sort of alliance with the Tsar. As soon as Astrakhan fell Ivan the Terrible decided on the foundation of the Fort Terka at the mouth of the Terek, and apparently accomplished this in 1560, when a Russian force attacked the Shevkal, in support of the Kabarda princes who were then at war with him. In 1561 Ivan married the daughter of Temriuk, the Kabarda prince. In 1577 the Russians built a new fort on the Sundzha River where it meets the Terek — that is, closer to Kabarda and better able to support it. From this time on the Russians continually claimed that the Kabardines had submitted to their rule. A Russian document of a century later lists the princes of the family that the Russians imagined ruled over Kabarda as monarchs, whereas actually they were simply the leading princes of a loose federation. In almost every case it runs as follows: 'Prince Mastriuk; the Tsar gave him the principality of Kabarda, but in Kabarda the principality was not given to him.'

In the 1570's the Turks were at war with Persia, and the Crimean armies supporting the Turks marched through the Kabarda territories, and were engaged in battle by the Persians and defeated. The Russians seem to have attacked the remnants of the Crimean army on its retreat. In 1588 they founded a new Terka in a better position than the older one, but nearby.

And in 1593 to 1594 the Caucasian wars of the Russians opened. These were to last three centuries. The Russian force was defeated by the Shevkal. In 1604–5 another attack was made on the Shevkal and again the Russians were defeated and had to abandon their advanced forts. For the rest of the century there was no forward movement on the part of the Russians.

By the 1720's the Persian state had virtually collapsed, and Peter the Great decided to conquer the Caspian provinces of Persia. The member of his council who advised him on this forward policy in the Caucasian area was the Tolstoy of the time, the ancestor of the writer who was himself later to serve in and write of such campaigns.

In 1722 Peter transported an army by sea from Astrakhan to the Daghestan coast, and occupied territory up to Baku. But the Persian power was re-established by the new dynasty of Nadir Shah and the Russians were gradually forced over the period 1729 to 1735 to abandon all the provinces they had annexed, including Derbent and Baku — which were not to return to Russian domination till the nineteenth century.

Thus in 1735 the Russians were in much the same position as they had been in the 1570's. They had a few forts and a few Cossack establishments on the Terek, and the Kabarda mountaineers, theoretically in submission to the Tsar, were in fact practically independent. Even the Treaty of Belgrade in 1739, after the next Turkish war, did not give the Russians many more rights in Kabarda than it gave the Turks.

In 1762 the Russians decided to extend their domination in the North Caucasus to the west. A new fort was founded, Mozdok, 250 miles up the Terek from Kizlyar. The Russo-Turkish war of 1768 resulted in the formal annexation of Kabarda by Russia — through the Treaty of Karsou between Russia and the Crimea signed in 1772. It took some time actually to enforce this. But in 1777 Catherine II approved a project for establishing the 'line of the Caucasus' — a series of military forts and Cossack settlements extending up the valley of the Terek to the Sea of Azov. The garrisons were formed by Cossacks transferred from the Lower Volga, and some regular troops. In 1779 Russian troops penetrated Kabarda, and at the end of the year the lords of Great and Little Kabarda made their submission. They were instructed to carry on under their own laws, but in 1791 an attempt was made to get them to elect their own 'judges', rather than leave justice to the traditional Islamic practitioners. In 1799 these elections were sabotaged and it was impossible to elect judges. Resistance continued over the beginning of the next century.

In 1775 the Russian troops entered Daghestan, without any considerable military success. The Shevkal accepted a protectorate in 1784. And it was fairly well established by a later treaty in 1793. In 1796 a large Russian expedition occupied both Daghestan and the Persian provinces as far as the Kura, and founded fortresses at Baku and elsewhere. The death of Catherine the Great and the accession of the Emperor Paul I in December 1796 led to the immediate recall of the Russian troops. And in 1796 all the Russians were back on the Terek except for a small contingent left in Georgia.

Georgia had collapsed into anarchy in the eighteenth century, when King Irakli succeeded in forming a fair-sized state in Central Georgia, round Tiflis. Other Georgian kings had solicited Russian help in 1768, and in 1769 General Todleben and a Russian military detachment had arrived to assist one of the minor Georgian kings. In 1771 these troops were recalled. But in 1783 Irakli was able to secure a treaty by which Russia guaranteed Georgia's territorial integrity, though Georgia accepted certain limitations on her conduct of foreign affairs. The Russians undertook to assist Irakli in reclaiming any territory that he felt was his. In 1795 a huge Persian army invaded Georgia and captured Tiflis. The following year the Russians undertook their invasion of Persia; some troops were sent to Georgia but left it in 1797.

Irakli died in 1798. In 1801 Paul I took the decision to annex Georgia, and in spite of various treaties and the demands of the Georgian negotiators, this was accomplished in the same year. Dynastic troubles and the threat from powerful Mohammedan neighbours made resistance to Russia abortive.

The races which sought Russian support against the Turks and Persians were the Christian Georgians (the Mohammedan Georgians remaining strongly anti-Russian) and the Christian (and Indo-European) Ossetians. And the Kabardines were already inclined to the Russian alliance. The Russian expansion therefore followed two routes. Physical geography made advance along the Caspian coast simple once the key point of Derbent had been taken — particularly as the Russians always had command of the sea on the Caspian, which they did not on the Black Sea until a late date. The other route depended on political geography as much as physical, lying through the territory of the Ossetians to the frontier of the Georgians, across what is now the Caucasian military highway, from Vladikavkaz to Tiflis, the key points for them here being secured by their allies. As we have seen, Georgia was annexed to Russia in 1801, and by 1828 almost the whole of the present Transcaucasia was Russian, leaving in the rear of it two large independent territories. On the eastern flank lay the Chechens, Ingushi and mountain Daghestani, and on the western the great stretch of Circassian Abkhazia protected in the north by the Turkish fortress of Anapa. And the Turks still held coastal Georgia as far as Poti.

In 1828–9 the Russians fought the first major Caucasian campaign against the Turks. Poti and Anapa were captured — the Russians at this time had command of the Black Sea owing to Navarino, an advantage they did not enjoy in the subsequent Caucasian wars. The Russians were victorious on the main front, where the major resistance came from Mohammedan Georgians, and they gained a certain amount of territory at the peace.

The two great Mohammedan centres behind the Russian lines were very different in character. The Circassians were ruled by great Beys and landowners and were in constant contact with Turkey. The Chechens and Ingushi who lived a more democratic life in their wild mountainous territory, had become attached to the puritan and egalitarian Muridist movement which somewhat resembled the contemporary Wahabi.

Moscow □

Frontier 1762
Annexed 1762-1783
Annexed 1783-1801
Annexed 1801-1830
Annexed 1830-1864

Dneor

Azov   *Don*

Volga

Ochakov

Astrakhan

Azov Sea

KHANATE OF THE CRIMEA

*Caspian
Sea*

Bakhchisarai   *Anapa*

Kizlyar

CIRCASSIA   *Mozdok*

Tarki

Vladikavkaz

BLACK   SEA   *Grozny*
CHECHNIYA

Tbilisi
GEORGIAN
KINGDOM

Baku

*Russia's Southward Expansion
1762 – 1864*

The Chechens had already come out on religious grounds
against the Russians in the Russo-Turkish war of 1769. In 1830,
the Murid, Imam Kazi Mullah, raised the country, already
irritated by punitive expeditions. Several Russian detachments
were destroyed, the Caucasian Line was pierced at several
points and towns beyond the Terek were raided. The Avars and
the other Daghestani tribes simultaneously threatened Derbent
and raided Georgia, and the Chechens made an attempt on
Vladikavkaz. The campaign following lasted three years before

the Russians captured Gimri, the Murid capital, and killed the Imam.

The next Imam was the famous Shamil, who revived the guerrilla war. In 1837 the Russians made a serious attempt to destroy both Circassian and Murid resistance. Russian forces suffered heavy losses on both fronts. They captured the main towns of Circassia, but in the Chechen mountains their progress was small. In 1840, the Circassians had stormed a number of Russian strongholds, but had been defeated and were in a difficult position, when the Murid danger made the Russians suspend operations in Circassia to concentrate all their forces against Shamil. He had inflicted heavy losses in various minor actions between 1840 and 1842. In 1843 the Muridists gained even bigger successes, including the capture of some forty guns, and attracted thousands of new recruits. The Russians were compelled to evacuate the whole of Chechnia and many points in Daghestan. They now concentrated 30,000 men and a large artillery force, the largest army that could be maintained in the area, against Shamil, and in 1845 the major attack was launched. It was an unmitigated disaster for the Russians, who lost 4,000 men and most of their baggage train in the famous Dargo campaign. Shamil now raided far and wide, but he was unable to make contact with the Circassians and was eventually forced with withdrawal to the mountains again.

When the Crimean War started in 1853 Shamil and the Circassians were both unsubdued. Shamil immediately raided Georgia and the Russians were compelled to divert large forces from the Turkish front. In 1854 the Turks landed forces in Abkhazia and the tribes there rose against the Russians. In the same year Shamil made a more serious attack on Georgia but was defeated. Turkish defeats on the main front were discouraging to both the Circassians and the Chechens and no co-ordinated action took place. In 1856, when the war ended, the Russians were able to concentrate their armies against the Chechens and Daghestanis just as after the previous war.

The fight against Shamil had now gone on for a quarter of a century and the Chechens were at the end of their resources.

In *Chechnia and the Chechens* (Tiflis, 1859) A.P. Berzhe says, 'In the subjugation of Chechnia, the population of Lesser Chechnia — the plains — was halved between 1847 and 1850, and by 1860 had been reduced to a quarter.'

In Circassia there had been continual trouble between the local population and the Russian settlers who had appropriated their land. By 1860, when the whole of the rest of the Caucasus had been subdued, there were still Circassians living in complete independence as far north as the Kuban River. A first attempt to make the Circassians emigrate to Turkey or to other regions of the Russian Empire was only partly successful and a new national Circassian government was set up in Sochi. But the Russian forces could now be concentrated against the Circassians and in 1862 the attack began. The fighting continued for two years and finally some 600,000 Circassians were expelled from their country and it was settled with Russian subjects.

Thus was carried out Nicholas I's order for 'the pacification once and for all of the mountain peoples, or the shooting of the disobedient'. The story of the émigré Circassians shows the remarkable unity of the Muslim world. They played an important part in many countries in the middle east. The Mamelukes, for instance, were Circassians not only in their origins but also in their recruitment. Their women were also celebrated throughout the harems of the area. And by this combination of sex and soldiering the race achieved great prominence. They are now scattered throughout the old Turkish Empire.

The reduction of the North Caucasus thus came half a century after Georgia to the south of it had accepted Russian rule. This resistance was, in fact, as bitter and determined as has ever been made — even leaving aside the military genius of Shamil. But the subdued peoples did not regard the matter as final. When Russia and Turkey again went to war in 1877 further revolts took place and in all six and a half Russian divisions had to be detached to the North Caucasus. The Turks again landed troops in Abkhazia and were supported by a major rising. In Chechnia a new Imam was proclaimed. The rising was temporarily suppressed, largely owing to the super-iority of the new Russian rifle, but it flared up again and was only put down after considerable fighting, and the Russians were forced to keep considerable forces in the area. Again Turkish defeats on the main front led to loss of enthusiasm among the rebels.

In 1905 there was trouble in Chechnia and in 1917 the collapse of the Tsarist regime led to the proclamation of a new Imam, Najmudin Gotsinski, and a more powerful figure, the Emir of Chechnia, Sheikh Uzun Hadji, who followed the Shamil tradition of theocratic democracy.

Such is a general account of how the Russians came into contact with the nations to the south of them, and finally conquered them. It is a story of a powerful military empire suppressing, with considerable difficulty, the desperate and ever-renewed resistance of peoples reluctant to give up their independence. The 1917 October revolution, it was often proclaimed, removed all these grievances of the non-Russian peoples and satisfied their national aspirations.

Chapter 2

IN THE MOUNTAINS

———◆◆◆◆◆———

Four of the nations we are dealing with inhabited the northern slopes of the Caucasus. They were the Chechens, the Ingushi, the Karachai and the Balkars. In numbers they comprised nearly half the total deportees. The Chechens were the largest single people to suffer deportation. With the closely related Ingushi, who formed part of the same Chechen-Ingush Autonomous Soviet Socialist Republic, they totalled just half a million in 1939 (Chechens 407,690, Ingushi 92,074). Partly for this reason I have often taken them as representative, when it is wished to illustrate some point which applies equally to all the deportees. Thus, in this chapter, certain themes are developed at some length which, to avoid repetition, are more briefly put in the case of nations sent into exile from other areas.

Lermontov begins *Princess Mary* — the main section of his *Hero of Our Own Times* — with a description of the Caucasian landscape as seen from Pyatigorsk, where the view southwards includes the stretch from Mount Elbruz, in the Karachai-Balkar country, to Mount Kazbek on the borders of Ingushetia:

May 11th. Yesterday I reached Pyatigorsk, and found rooms just inside the town on high ground at the foot of Mashuk. If rough weather comes, the clouds will lap my roof. When I opened the window at five o'clock this morning, the room was filled with the scent of flowers that were growing in the little front garden. Branches of cherry blossom peer in at the window, and the wind sometimes scatters the white petals over my writing-table. The view in three directions is splendid. Westward are the five blue peaks of Beshtu, looking (to quote Pushkin) like the vestiges of a scattered thunderstorm. To the north the horizon is blocked by

Mashuk, which resembles a Persian fur-cap. The eastern prospect is comparatively gentle, for below me here lies the clean, new-built town, from which rise the murmur of the medicinal springs and the voices of the cosmopolitan crowd. Beyond, the hills, blue and hazy in the distance, form an amphitheatre, fringed by the silvery chain of the snows that stretch from Mount Kazbek to the twin summits of Elbruz.

It is delightful to live in such a place. An agreeable feeling pervades my whole body. The air is pure and fresh as a child's kiss. The sun shines brightly, and there is not a cloud to dim the sky . . .

Such, in one of the many fine descriptions of it in Russian literature, is the area where the Chechens, the Ingushi, the Karachai and the Balkars lived among the group of little nations whose homelands lie in the northern sweep of the great mountain chain.

At first sight the ethnology of the Northern Caucasus is an almost incomprehensible puzzle. But we can deal with it quite simply. In the first place we can ignore for the purposes of this book the most complex area — multinational Daghestan. That leaves us, strung along between the Daghestan frontier on the south-east and the Adygei Autonomous Province to the north-west, four linguistic groups:

(a) Turkic — the Karachai and Balkars

(b) Iranian — the Ossetians

(c) the Chechens and Ingushi

(d) the Adygei (Circassian) of which different dialects form the speech of the Adygei Autonomous Province, of the former Cherkess Autonomous Province, and of the Kabardines.

(c) and (d) are distantly connected, and are purely Caucasian, having no representatives outside the area.

It will be seen that the deportees, from this part, consisted of groups (a) and (c). The Christianized and Indo-European speaking Ossetians have always been pro-Russian; while the Circassian groups are historically the pro-Russian rump of a larger nation now mainly dispersed.

Although national characteristics in the North Caucasus

seem so divisive, there has always been a degree of unity among at least the Mohammedan races there. We find in the Caucasian stories of Lermontov and Tolstoy the non-Turkic nations speaking 'Tatar' as a lingua franca — as for instance the Kabardines in Lermontov's *Bela*. (The dialect in general use was Kumyk, a Turkic language of Daghestan.) Tolstoy's stories of the Caucasian campaign, in which he himself served, show, time and again, the unity in action among the mountain peoples achieved by the Murids: three or four nationalities, again speaking 'Tatar' amongst themselves, are found together in raiding parties. G. J. Georgi, writing in the 1790's, describes the Caucasian tribes separately, but also puts them all together under the heading 'Mountain Tatar'. Later writers use this term to cover the Karachai, the Balkars, the Ingushi, the Chechens, and the Abazins and Kumyks of Daghestan.

The conquest of the Caucasus has always been for Russian nationalism most significant and symbolic in the imagination, far more so than the annexations in Central Asia and in the Far East. Raising the symbols of Russian imperial power on the great mountains has been highly regarded as a demonstration of might, and exalted as such by those Russians who admire such a thing. Of course, a large country's manifest destiny to rule other areas may thrill its own nationals, but it is less likely to appeal to the local inhabitants. The idea of the 'Russian Caucasus' appears in the poets and novelists who came to the area — in Pushkin, Lermontov and even Tolstoy. As Mr. Kolarz says, in Lermontov particularly the idea of the Caucasus is interpreted as 'a whole period of Russian history and a political programme strongly flavoured with romanticism.' Lermontov did indeed regret the passing of the free life of the mountaineers but he prophesied (wrongly as it turned out) that the Circassians would be proud to say, 'we may truly be slaves, but at least we are slaves of the ruler of the universe!' Pushkin too treated the subjection of the mountaineers as a historical necessity. In his *Caucasian Prisoner* even though speaking of the Russian General Kotlyarevski as 'the scourge of the Caucasus . . . .Your way, like a black plague, lost and anni-

The Pre-deportaion Ethnography of the North Caucasus

Mongol (Kalmyk)
Iranian (Ossetian)
Caucasian { Avar
{ Chechen-Ingush
Circassian (Adygei, Cherkess, Kabardine, Abkhaz)
Turkic (Karachai, Balkar, Nogai, Kumyk)

hilated tribes', he exalts the conquest and calls on the Caucasus to 'tremble, for Yermolov comes'.

This is not the place for a complete description of the customs and ways of life of the North Caucasian nations, and it will be sufficient if the reader envisages mountaineers, intensely loyal to Mohammedanism in its most egalitarian forms, quick to resent injury, intelligent, and devoted to their independence. In the valleys a skilled and specialized agriculture was practised, with special repute for orchards and bee-keeping. Many of the *auls* or villages were fortified strong-points on the spurs of the mountains. Beyond lay the great forests into which the warrior groups could retreat from the Russian artillery. Flocks pastured on the higher slopes, to which, for instance, the shepherd nation of Balkars was virtually confined.

When Yermolov established his greatest fortress, Grozny — 'the Terrible'—it was in the Chechen territory and was designed to overawe that largest and most martial of the mountain nations. The Chechens and Ingushi have evidently been in the Caucasus for several millennia, resisting the efforts of a series of long-lived but nevertheless mortal empires to destroy them. It was left to Stalin to attempt finally to eradicate this ancient race from its ancient home.

National tradition has the Chechens descend from the legendary hero Turpalo-Nokhchou. A song about him, surviving in our own times, is quoted in the book *On the Basic Problems of Chechnia* (Grozny, 1930):

> Like sparks struck from steel
> We sprang from Turpalo-Nokhchou.
> We were born in the night
> When the she-wolf bore her litter.
> We will not lose the glory
> Of the name of our father
> Turpalo-Nokhchou.

The ideal of the Chechens — and by and large of all the mountaineers — was the *dzhigit* — equivalent of the Homeric 'hero' or the Amerindian 'brave', but always associated too with the idea of fine horsemanship.

There are many descriptions of the Chechens, some by English travellers, in the earlier part of the nineteenth century. They mainly dwell on their qualities as raiders and fighters. A more essential point is brought out by a French anthropologist, Ernest Chantre, writing in 1887:

> In the days of their independence the Chechens were grouped in separate communities administered by a National Assembly. Today they constitute a single people having no consciousness of class distinctions. In this they are very different from the Circassians, among whom the nobility has a dominating position. There is a very sharp contrast between the aristocratic form of the Circassian Republic and the essentially democratic constitution of the Chechens and the peoples of Daghestan . . . Among the inhabitants of the eastern Caucasus there is complete equality. The powers with which they invest their elected Elders in Council are limited both in time and in extent . . . The Chechens are gay and intelligent. The Russian officers call them the French of the Caucasus.

It was this egalitarianism that went with the desperate resistance to Tsarist conquest, recognized by the Russian soldiery themselves — as in *A Hero of Our Own Times* where Lermontov has a veteran describing the Chechens as people, 'who, though robbers and rogues, are at any rate desperate blades'. The soldier goes on to say:

> Well, old man, they were cut-throats there, if you like! Now, thanks be, the times are peaceful; but I've seen the days when, if you went a hundred paces outside the walls you'd come across a shaggy devil on watch, and you had to keep your eyes skinned if you didn't want to get a lasso round your neck or a bullet in the back of your head. Fine fellows, they were!

Lermontov writes of another mountaineer:

> I've seen some of them at work, cut all to pieces, riddled like a sieve with bayonet wounds, but they go on using their swords as if there were nothing the matter.

The smaller Ingushi nation, recognized as no less liberty-loving than their neighbours from the time when their semi-legendary forbear Kertskhal founded Nazran, right up to their Borovoye revolt in the deportation area in 1945, was also thought of as a virtuous people. In his *Ingushi* (Moscow, 1925), for instance, Prof. N. Yakovlev quotes an unnamed researcher of the previous century to the effect that 'the Ingushi are less inclined than the others to robbery; they are respected as good and honest people.'

The Ingushi lived in the western strip of the republic, with Nazran as their main town. Their mountain *auls* are specially known for the defensive towers or turrets which dominate them. But their territory is on the whole less defensible than that of Chechnia proper, and they have been subjected to the Georgians, in the eleventh century, and the Kabardines in the fifteenth, apart from the later conqueror. They always offered strenuous resistance.

Lermontov describes the *dzhigits* as they appeared to the outside observer. Tolstoy goes to the heart of the matter when he recounts the motives of Chechen-Ingush irreconcilability. In his *Hadji Murad* he describes a Russian Army raid on a village of the Chechens. Houses, trees and hay are burnt, children killed, and the fountain and the mosque polluted. When the Chechens return from the mountains where they had taken refuge:

> No one spoke of hatred of the Russians. The feeling experienced by all the Chechens, from the youngest to the oldest, was stronger than hate. It was not hatred, for they did not regard those Russian dogs as human beings, but it was such repulsion, disgust, and perplexity at the senseless cruelty of these creatures, that the desire to exterminate them — like the desire to exterminate rats, poisonous spiders, or wolves — was as natural an instinct as that of self-preservation.
>
> The inhabitants of the *aul* were confronted by the choice of remaining there and restoring with frightful effort what had been produced with such labour and had been so lightly and senselessly destroyed, facing every moment the possibility of a repetition of what had happened; or to submit to the Russians — contrary to their religion and despite the repulsion and contempt they felt for them. The old men prayed, and unanimously decided to send envoys to Shamil asking him for help.

This may stand for the whole resistance of the nations of the conquered periphery of Russia, unquenched to this day.

In the early days of the Soviet regime a good view was taken of the Chechens, and their history was presented in a favourable light. The first edition of the *Large Soviet Encyclopaedia* has long articles on the Chechens and Chechnia and may be quoted as typical of the then Soviet view of the Tsarist conquest. It is interesting in several respects — in comparison with what was said later about the progressive nature of Tsarist annexation, in condemning strongly actions later carried out by the Communists in their turn, and in giving certain details which, to avoid repetition, have not been brought into the brief historical summary in Chapter I.

After mentioning that among the Chechens 'Feudal relations . . . were not developed', the article goes on:

> An extraordinary stubborn struggle with the settlers of Tsarism was carried on by the mountaineers from the end of the eighteenth century (1785–1859). The most active and powerful opponents of the Tsarist government of the conquest of Northern Caucasia may justly be considered to be the Chechens. The pressure of Tsarist forces on the mountaineers brought about their unity in the struggle for their independence. And in this struggle of the mountaineers the Chechens played the most distinguished role, providing the main fighting forces and supplies for the Gazava (Holy Wars). Chechnia was the 'granary' of the Gazava.

The article goes on to describe the rise of the Mansur Ushurma, the first Imam, who fought the Russians for six years (1785–91), and his successor Kazi Mullah. It then deals with the greatest of Caucasian heroes, Shamil:

> But the struggle reached its greatest force in the epoch of the remarkable leader of the mountaineers, Shamil (1834–59) who, basing himself on a broad national movement, was able brilliantly to organize the active resistance to Tsarism, not only by force of his military talents, but also by force of the social and political reforms carried out by him.

In the course of the war

> The generals of Nicholas, after a series of defeats, realized that the way to defeat the mountaineers lay through Chechnia. There began a methodic squeezing out of the Chechens by roads through the valleys, the destruction of villages, the chopping down of

woods, the construction of fortresses and the resettlement of the
'liberated lands' by Cossack stanitzas. The people, ruined by
war, deprived of half their best lands, were still not defeated
(1859). As a culmination the most vital elements of the population
were deported to Turkey to the number of over 20,000, and were
in fact destined in their majority to dying out (1865). But
Chechnia seethed: in 1867 there broke out the powerful rising
of the Kuata-Hadjintsi. Chechnia rose again in 1877 in connection with the Russo-Turkish war. The risings drew on themselves cruel executions and masses of victims, the annihilation of
auls and the destruction of crops.

The article goes on to speak of later years and

the systematic expropriation of the mountain lands continued
after the subjugation of the mountaineers. The lands of the
Chechens were distributed to Cossacks, military and civil officials,
who had taken part in the subjugation of Chechnia, and others.

In addition 'in order to weaken the subjugated people, the
government carried out the transfer of the most restive of the
population', and in particular those from 'inaccessible mountain areas', to places where the Russian government would
more easily be able to 'set up supervision of them'. The article
tells how they became economically exploited, with the result
that in the 1905 revolution they made 'armed attempts' to
reclaim their lands. The result was 'more executions and the
deportation of hundreds of families to Siberia'.

The general theme of this article (which it has been thought
worth quoting at some length as typical of what was said until
fairly recently about minority history) is the same as that of
various shocked references to Tsarist oppression made by high
Soviet authority, and especially by Stalin himself. In his classic
on nationality matters he says:

The old government, the landlords and the capitalists have left
us as a heritage such browbeaten peoples as . . . the Chechens. . . .
These peoples were doomed to incredible suffering and to
extinction. (Stalin, *Marxism and the National and Colonial Question*,
p. 104, London, 1947.)

And again, in the *Thesis on the National Question* presented by
Lenin to the tenth Congress of the Russian Communist Party,
it is stated that

These 10,000,000 individuals, Kirghiz, Bashkirs, Chechens, Ossetians, Ingushi, were right up till recently, methodically dispossessed of their best lands by Russian colonists. Driven gradually into sterile deserts these people were devoted to certain death. (*Life of the Nationalities*, 13–2.)

The next twenty-five years were to prove an ironic commentary on this theme.

AFTER THE REVOLUTION

At the time of the Revolution many promises were made to the minority peoples, and often by name to those later deported. Only the week after the seizure of power the Soviet government issued a *Declaration of Rights of the Peoples of Russia* (still declared to be the basis of Communist national policy, as in the *Large Soviet Encyclopaedia*, 2nd edition, vol. 24, p. 292) which went to the length of admitting the right of subject races to express their wishes by rebellion:

If any nation whatsoever is retained as part of a given State by force, if, despite its expressed desire — whether expressed in the press, in popular assemblies, in the decisions of political parties, *or by rebellions and insurrections against national oppression* [my italics] it has not the right of choosing freely — the troops of the annexing or, generally the more powerful nation being completely withdrawn and without any pressure being brought to bear — the constitutional forms of its national existence, then its incorporation is an annexation, that is, seizure and coercion. (*Collection of Decrees and Regulations of the Workers' and Peasants' Government*, No. 2, 1917, Article 18.)

Soon afterwards the government issued an appeal, signed by Lenin:

Moslems of Russia, Tatars of the Volga and the Crimea, Kirghiz and Sarts of Siberia and Turkestan, Turks and Tatars of Trans-Caucasia, Chechens and mountain Cossacks! All you, whose mosques and shrines have been destroyed, whose faith and customs have been violated by the Tsars and oppressors of Russia! Henceforward your beliefs and customs, your national and cultural institutions are declared free and inviolable! Build your national life freely and without hindrance. It is your right. Know that your rights, like those of all the peoples of Russia, will be protected by the might of the Revolution, by the councils of

c

Workers', Soldiers', and Peasants' Deputies! (*Collection of Decrees and Regulations of the Workers' and Peasants' Government*, No. 6, December 19th, 1917, Appendix 2e.)

The article on the Chechen Autonomous Province in the first edition of the *Large Soviet Encyclopaedia*, already referred to, gives a partisan account of Chechnia in the Revolution, which yet presents much of the reality of the struggle which now took place in the mountains.

At first 'labouring Chechnia did not stand finally on the road of Soviet power' on account of a period of 'bourgeois nationalist movements, under the leadership of "their own" sheikhs, kulaks and capitalists'. These set up 'at the beginning of the February revolution, in Grozny, a Chechen Congress, which elected a national committee of sheikhs, officers and merchants'. In May a 'Mountain Congress' in Vladikavkaz was also taken part in by the 'reactionary nationalist elements of Chechnia'. This set up a 'Central Committee of the Union of Mountaineers' of a bourgeois-feudal character. Moreover the 'chauvinist counter-revolutionary leaders turned the Chechens against Russians in general' influencing 'the peasant masses and sometimes even the workers (through Mensheviks and S.R's. taking part in the Grozny Soviet) among the Chechens'. The Chechens armed themselves in every way. Units recalled from the Wild Division brought their weapons.

Detachments of 'self-defenders' falling under the control of kulaks and sheikhs (Ali Mitaev and others), disarmed soldiers returning from the Caucasian Front, and seized weapons left in fortresses by soldiers of the garrisons who had returned from there to the motherland (Vedeno, Vozdvizhenka). In this period there took place mass attacks by Chechens against the Cossack stanitsas and at the same time attacks by the Cossacks on the Chechen auls . . . In the middle of November 1917, a formal battle took place between units of the Chechen regiment and Russians, mainly Cossack units, which finished in a mass pogrom of the Chechens in Grozny, who in their turn raised the cry of nationalism in Chechnia. At the head of the national committee stood the reactionary sheikh Deni Arsanov. The town was surrounded. In their turn the inhabitants of Grozny dug themselves in. . . .

Sheikh Arsanov himself, while attempting negotiations about peace with the Cossack leaders was surprised and annihilated by them with all his band of Murids, fifty in all, in Grozny station. A second episode from these days: when units of the 111th regiment, in charge of the Vozdvizhenka fortress, were demobilized, leaving it and returning to their country, the Chechens from neighbouring auls took the fortress, destroyed the barracks and churches and other stone buildings, expelled the Russian inhabitants to Grozny and themselves settled the place.

The *Encyclopaedia* continues:

At the end of 1917 the leaders of the Cossacks of the Mozdok Province in congress, attempted to create a bloc of all Russians against the Chechens and Ingushis, declaring themselves to be on the side of the Soviet power. This provocational tactic was unmasked only by the small, but influential, Bolshevik delegation to the congress (Kirov and others). The Central Committee of the Union of United Mountaineers openly joined the counter-revolutionaries, the so-called South-eastern Union of Cossack Armies, Mountaineers of the Caucasus and Free Peoples of the Steppe.

In January 1918, the article goes on, 'a so-called "Atagoi Soviet" was organized in Chechnia, in which the predominating influence was obtained by the priesthood and kulaks standing on the positions of zoological nationalism'. However, this body was finally, by a series of developments and splits, turned into an organization supporting the Soviet regime. What in fact seems to have happened is fairly simple; when the Chechens thought that the Cossacks and Russians were pro-Soviet they themselves became anti-Soviet. As soon as the counter-revolutionary movement started winning over the local Russians and Cossacks the Chechens turned to the other side.

'A most important role among the pioneers of the Soviet movement in Chechnia was played by Sergo Ordzhonikidze . . .' and by February 1918, the article continues, 'a leading local Communist, A. Sheripov, declared that the overwhelming majority of the Chechen people was ready to fight for the Soviet power'. Sheripov headed 'Chechen units of the Red Army' which 'took part in the battles of the Grozny workers against the Cossack counter-revolutionaries'. Severe fighting took place, and 'in February 1919 the Soviet forces left Grozny'. The White armies were by this time fully organized and in control of most of South Russia. The Chechens continued to fight them in the mountains. 'Hundreds and thousands of poor Chechens devotedly fought against the White Guard regiments and artillery, suffering heavy losses'. The *Encyclopaedia* claims Bolshevik leadership for some of this resistance, but admits that 'a new movement of labouring Chechnia was called up. But at first the masses were under the flag of the Shariya'.

The Shariya, the Islamic system of law and custom which had been implicitly guaranteed by the Appeal of December 1917, is here treated as a hostile influence. But at the time Stalin stated directly, with specific reference to the Chechens and Ingushi and the other mountain peoples:

> If it is shown that the Shariya is necessary, then let the Shariya remain. The Soviet Government has no thought of declaring war on the Shariya. (Stalin, *Works*, Vol. 4, Foreign Languages Publishing House, Moscow, 1953, p. 415.)

To return to the *Encyclopaedia*, it describes the movement based on Islamic and national feeling which now arose:

> The movement was headed by the fanatical sheikh, well known in the mountains, Uzun-Hadji, Imam and Emir of the North Caucasian Emirate . . . Uzun-Hadji opened active war against the army of Denikin, and a 'united front' of its own sort was proposed to him by the leaders of Soviet Chechnia, Sheripov and Gikalo, in this struggle against Denikin, with the preservation of wholly independent red units. At the same time they did not give up their work of unmasking the social face of Uzun-Hadji. The movement was so important that the Denikinists were compelled to detach large forces to the Chechen front.

The *Encyclopaedia* goes on to describe a struggle for influence between the Bolsheviks and Uzun-Hadji with the result that, not unnaturally, the 'Uzun-Hadjist movement showed its true face . . . carrying out policies openly hostile to the Bolsheviks'. The 'bourgeois nationalists' were still, however, fighting in collaboration with Red units in September 1919, and it was only on January 31st, 1920 that the leaders 'showed their counter-revolutionary face' and then only by failing to assist a

small Communist force attacked by a larger White unit. Open
fighting broke out shortly afterwards and at first the Communists had to retreat into Georgia. But 'in March 1920, in
Chechnia, Soviet power was finally celebrated'.

Though this account, to put it mildly, requires supple-
menting from other sources, it gives a fair impression of the
main moves in the struggle for power in the mountains, and
indicates pretty plainly the essence of the matter: that the
Chechens and Ingushi were the mainstay of the struggle
against the Whites, that they were at first prepared to take the
Bolsheviks at their face value, that they then became dis-
illusioned and went into open opposition, and that they were
subdued from outside. That the Ingushi, in particular, had
supported the Bolsheviks wholeheartedly at the critical moment
was gratefully admitted by Ordzhonikidze, the Bolshevik
leader in the area, in a speech in December 1918:

> I recall the moment . . . when our fate hung on a hair; this
> was a moment . . . when we had no following . . . when we were
> looked upon with timidity . . . when only the Ingushi followed us
> without hesitation. (*Soviet Republics in the North Caucasus in 1918*,
> I, Borisenko, Rostov, 1930, Vol. 2, pp. 72–3.)

The post-revolution organization of the North Caucasus
split the area in two. The mountain tribes of Daghestan were
united with the Russified plain stretching up to and north of
the Terek River. The Chechens and Ingushi, whose closest ties
were with the Avars in mountain Daghestan, were detached
from them and united with the other nations to the north-
westward. This second republic — 'the Mountain Republic' —
united the Chechens, Ingushi, Ossetians, Kabardines, Balkars
and Karachai. Each of these six nations formed a district,
Stalin having said:

> Each of these peoples — Chechens, Ingushi, Ossetians, Kabar-
> dines, Balkars, Karachai, and also the Cossacks who remain
> within the autonomous mountain territory — should have its
> National Soviet to administer the affairs of the given people in
> accordance with its manner of life. (Stalin, *Works*, English
> edition, Moscow, 1953, Vol. 4, p. 415.)

The towns of Grozny and Vladikavkaz were given separate status.

In April 1921, a congress took place at Vladikavkaz after which a telegram was sent to Stalin, Commissar for Nationalities, saying that 'liberated from the yoke of the oppressor the mountaineers of the Caucasus, Chechens, Ingushi, Ossetians, Dighors, Balkars and Karachai on this memorable day are all animated with the ardent desire to finally conquer world imperialism which holds in slavery millions of orientals'. The executive committee of thirteen members set up seems to have contained nine Russians, two from the always pro-Russian Ossetians, one Ingush and one of doubtful nationality.

The history of the Mountain A.S.S.R. may be briefly stated in terms of the elements into which it was broken up. In September 1921 Kabarda was removed from it and turned into an autonomous province. In January 1922 the Karachai were taken from it and given a joint autonomous province with the Cherkess, with a capital at Batalpashinsk: at the same time the Balkars were merged into a Kabardino-Balkar autonomous province with Nalchik for capital. In December 1922 the Chechens were given an autonomous province of their own. This left only the Ossetians and the Ingushi who were separated in July 1924, thus completing the disintegration of the Republic. Further changes were the breaking up of the Karachai-Cherkess autonomous province into two in April 1926 and the re-unification of the Chechens and Ingushi into a single province in January 1934. In December 1936 the Kabardino-Balkar, Chechen-Ingush and North Ossetian provinces became Autonomous Republics.

The mountain peoples had had a considerable amount of troubles amongst themselves at various times in their history. Nevertheless, when left alone they had shown a surprising capacity for unity. Shamil had been welcomed throughout the area, except by the Christian Ossetians. In 1917–20 all these nations had found it possible to co-operate in a single political unit. And the Soviet Government had originally recognized the advantages in setting up the Mountain Republic. That form of organization had, indeed, a progressive air to it. And the federation of the small peoples might have been expected to give a broader local loyalty than the division which later came into force.

The Soviet authorities, on the other hand, soon abandoned federal solutions in complicated national areas. The main case of this was the dissolution in 1936 of the Transcaucasian Soviet Federal Socialist Republic, which had united Georgia, Armenia and Azerbaijan. The erection one by one of all the Turkic nations of Turkestan into separate Union Republics had something of the same effect. What happened in all these cases was that local unity was halted and the administration of each area was linked direct to Moscow, so that there could be no question of any joint opposition on Party or Governmental level against the proposals of the Soviet Government, and no development of local solidarity in any way. Moreover local cultural unities were broken up where they existed. The idea of a unified Turki language in Central Asia was greatly discouraged and each local dialect was differentiated as far as possible from that of its neighbours, while at the same time being Russianized. In the North Caucasus there was no linguistic unity, but such elements of it as existed were discouraged. The languages generally understood in the North Caucasus were Turkic (Kumyk Tatar) on the one hand, and (in connection with the religious schools) Arabic, to a lesser extent, on the other. Soviet education has concentrated on substituting Russian as the tongue in which the Circassian speaks to the Chechen, just as it is through Moscow that he must make his political approach to members of the neighbouring nations.

In the years between the revolution and the deportation, Soviet sources are less inclined to refer to the scale of the troubles which continually flared up in the mountains. The resistance of 'kulak and mullah elements' to collectivization and to Soviet national policy, is mentioned occasionally. And more may be guessed from such references as this to the resistance to comparatively mild changes like the (temporary) introduction of the Latin alphabet in the late twenties:

> The same resistance to latinization emanated also from the home-bred sheikhs, murids and mullahs in Daghestan and among the mountain peoples of North Caucasia. The latter, led by Sheikh Ali Mitaev, drawing on the services of their hirelings (bandit elements) met literally with daggers drawn the first copies of the Soviet alphabets in the new script which appeared in the mountain villages. The hunger strike proclaimed by the Chechen mullahs in protest against latinization was a characteristic token of this opposition.
>
> We observe, too, the same scene of counter-action on the part of Ibrahim Valiev's supporters in the Crimea, who in every way sabotaged and tried to discredit the idea of latinization. (*Revolutsiya i Natsionalnosti*, No. 7, 1930, pp. 23–4.)

There were many complaints of the influence of Islam — that, for instance, the Ingushi, including many members of the Communist Party, were completely under Islamic influence, even the children refusing to touch atheist textbooks (*Antireligioznik*, No. 11, 1931).

That these changes were enforced by Russian officials is also clear from complaints like the following, which were occasionally allowed to appear in those days:

> In the apparatus of the Chechen Ingush Regional Executive Committee are officials who know neither the Chechen nor the Ingush language. (*Revolutsiya i Natsionalnosti*, No. 12, 1935, pp. 66–7.)

A decree of January 7th, 1936, reveals that of 1,310 officials in the North Caucasus territory, only 17 were of the mountain nationalities. This led to misunderstandings, which are given as part of the reason why the local soviets in Chechnia failed to carry out government orders (*Revolutsiya i Natsionalnosti*, No. 72, November 1931). Troubles had become so acute that Kalinin in person paid a visit and urged reconciliation (*Revolutsiya i Natsionalnosti*, No. 50, April 1934).

The idea of the North Caucasus which remained in the minds of the Stalinists may be seen from statements made at the trial of Bukharin and others in 1938. Evidence was given by V. I.

Ivanov, who had been Second Secretary in the North Caucasus in 1928–31, that he had acted there as an agent of the Rightist opposition. Bukharin, he said, had told him that 'the Northern Caucasus would play a very important part in our struggle against the Party and the Soviet power' and again 'we must make it our task to transform the Northern Caucasus into a Russian Vendée'. The formation of insurrectionary bands is also mentioned (*Report of the Court Proceedings in the Case of the Anti-soviet Bloc of Rights and Trotskyites*, English edition, Moscow, 1938, pp. 118–21). In his evidence Rykov, former Prime Minister of the Soviet Union, also mentioned the plotters' 'special attention to the North Caucasus' because *inter alia* of 'the specific character of its traditions and also in view of its political and economic importance as a region bordering on the Ukraine, possessing a large number of national republics and supplying a large quantity of grain'. He refers also to 'kulak insurrections' (op. cit., pp. 164–6).

These remarks, which we may take as having been drafted by the regime propagandists to put into the mouths of the accused, seem to indicate official sensitivity about the North Caucasus, and also give the impression that the strong peasant resistance being shown at the time throughout the U.S.S.R. was particularly powerful among the mountaineers. In drawing attention to the vulnerable nature of the area from a Soviet point of view, they seem to some extent to foreshadow the reasons for the eventual decision to deport the inhabitants.

The great majority of Soviet statements about the mountaineers, however, are ones which assert their loyalty and happiness. For completeness, we may quote a few of these. The *Encyclopaedia* article already referred to concludes:

> The Soviet power gave Chechnia autonomy, gave it literature, constructed tens of new schools, educated in technical and higher educational institutions hundreds of thousands of young people of the mountain poor, involved thousands of Chechen peasants in industry, creating qualified cadres of the Chechen proletariat. The Chechen Autonomous Province, overcoming the resistance of kulak and mullah elements, who used in the struggle aristocratic connections and religious prejudices, successfully

carried out the basic tasks facing the whole country — indus-
trialization, the creation of kolkhozes — and convincingly went
forward on the road of constructing a Socialist commonwealth.

In the last years of peace, on January 15th, 1939, *Izvestia*
published the following communiqué from the Tass agency:

Fifth anniversary of Checheno-Ingushetia. Grozny. 14th
January. Five years ago today, on 15th January 1934, two
Caucasian peoples, the Chechens and the Ingushi, closely
connected by their language, culture and way of life, joined
together to form the autonomous province of the Chechen-
Ingushi. On 5th December 1936, this province was converted
into an Autonomous Soviet Socialist Republic. The history of
Checheno-Ingushetia has been marred by decades of bloody
struggle on the part of a race with a strong love of liberty against
colonizers and the national bourgeoisie, the mainstay of Czarism.
But under the Soviet regime the republic has been so transformed
as to be unrecognizable. The kolkhozes, within which 92·7 per
cent of all agricultural undertakings are now combined, have
been accorded a perpetual grant of more than 400,000 hectares
of land. An important oil industry has been created. New oilfields
have been exploited and two big refineries built, as well as a
machine factory. Food factories, chemical factories and other
forms of local production have been brought into being or
organized. Under the sun of the Stalin Constitution the culture
of the Chechen-Ingush people, national in form but socialist in
content, has made a great step forward. Before the Revolution
there were only three schools in the whole of Checheno-
Ingushetia. Today there are 342 primary and secondary schools
accommodating 118,000 pupils. Hundreds of engineers and
teachers emerge every year from the high schools, the technical
schools and the workers' faculties. All these brilliant results have
been achieved in the course of a bitter struggle against the enemies
of the people — Trotskyites, Bukharinites and bourgeois nationalists who have sought to rob the workers of the fruits of the great
October Socialist Revolution.

This expression 'national in form, socialist in content' has
become a classic compression, much used in the U.S.S.R. to
express the essence of Soviet national policy. It has been
cynically translated as 'the right to say what the Kremlin wants
you to in your own language'. On political matters this is
demonstrably the case. But it is also true that one of the most

characteristic things in the life of the Soviet minorities is the
care taken to provide them with a Soviet literature of their own.
We will find that all the deported nations had a flourishing
production of poems — sometimes even 'folk poems' — praising
the regime, collective farms, the Party and, in particular,
Stalin personally. On this point, as on others, we may give a
single Chechen poem, in full, as typical of the sort of thing to
be found everywhere, but hardly bearing repetition. Here it
is:

CHECHEN SONG OF STALIN

Even if the sea were ink,
And the sky were made of paper
Who could tell the people's gladness,
Though inspired with highest fervour?
Who could express with faltering pen
Our love for you, Desired One.
Too small are the heavens and the oceans
To reveal the thoughts we hold.
You, our father and our brother,
Gave us happiness and opened
Wide the gates to future joy.
— Long life to you, beloved Stalin!
Such is our hope and prayer for you.
As the nacre hides its treasure,
Holy is the womb that bore thee.
Most happy is she above all women,
Whose child is our unfailing sun.
Like the stars so brightly shining,
You shine like the sun for us.
Your glory, spread among all peoples,
Is loudly hymned from land to land.
Stalin gave joy to us, his children,
Stalin — the dew in a thirsty land.
Flowers adorn the hills and meadows,
Flower of our hearts, — no less than these.
You, our father and our brother,
Gave us happiness, and opened
Wide the gates to future joy.
— Long life to you, beloved Stalin!
Such is our hope and prayer for you.
If the foe again should sharpen

His blade against the Soviet land
We shall not sleep. Just speak the word
And we shall rend them all like tigers.
Fresher than dewdrops, sweet as honey,
The Caucasus, its youth restored,
Comes to you, its people sing:
The name Stalin gleams like a star!
You, our father and our brother,
Gave us happiness and opened
Wide the gates to future joy.
— Long life to you, beloved Stalin!
Such is our hope and prayer for you.

(Translated from pp. 78–9,
Chechen-Ingush Folklore, Moscow, 1940.)

Unlike the Chechens and Ingushi, the Karachai and Balkars are not of the oldest indigenous stock. They arrived in the area from the Crimean sphere, as part of the Tatar wanderings of that time, about five hundred years ago. They were gradually driven by their larger neighbours into the alpine meadows and torrent valleys, close under the mountain glaciers, which they now mainly inhabit. To the south, at the watershed, the passes are at from 9,000–11,000 feet. The route from Klukhori into Georgia was nevertheless an old trade route in Byzantine times, though lately little used. They live mainly by sheep and cattle herding, and hunting.

Though of different stock the Karachai and Balkars had much the same history as their co-religionists, the Chechens and Ingushi. They too had offered stubborn resistance to the Tsars, especially in the 1820's, and they too had supported the Murids. And in general all that has been said about the Chechen-Ingush could be repeated about these small Turkic peoples.

The dialects of the Karachai and the Balkars are very similar, and on the basis of them a literary language — Karachai-Balkar — was developed in the twenties, when the authorities were upgrading the local Turkic dialects throughout the Union, with a view to helping prevent the rise, or the continuation, of a general Turkic sense of unity.

Though the Karachai and the Balkars live in geographical contiguity, they are separated by the mountains. Such separation has not prevented administrative unification in some other parts of the Soviet Union. For instance, a comparison of the ethnographical, physical and administrative maps of Ferghana Valley in Turkestan shows that, while ethnographical frontiers have to some extent been ignored, this has not been for reasons of physical geography; and that areas divided from one another by a series of physical barriers are nevertheless united to relatively inaccessible, rather than to their nearest units. The same, indeed, may be seen in a less striking way in the Caucasus itself, where the Nakhichevan A.S.S.R., with a Turkic population, forms part of Azerbaijan from which it is separated not merely by mountains, but actually by a broad strip of Armenian territory.

The Balkars were, up to the time of their deportation, neither given a separate territory nor united with the Karachai. Instead they formed part of the Kabardino-Balkar A.S.S.R. with the non-Turkic Kabardines. The total population of the republic in 1939 was 359,000, which indicates that Kabardines (and Russians) were in the great majority.

That the administrative convenience of uniting Balkars and Kabardines was not overwhelming is shown by the fact that for a time in the 1920's Balkaria formed part of the Mountain Republic while Kabarda did not, and also by the fact that when the Balkars were deported in 1944 much of their territory was not then united to Kabarda, but transferred to Georgia — although the mountain division between Balkaria and Georgia is at least as high and as difficult to cross as that between Balkaria and the Karachai.

Volume 4 of the first edition of the *Large Soviet Encyclopaedia* (1926) has short articles on the Balkars and Balkaria in which the people are described as shepherds and the country defined as 'the valley of the upper course of the Cherek — in a broad sense, the whole of the southern mountain part of the Kabardine-Balkar Autonomous Province'. Volume 30 (published in 1937) has an article on the Kabardine-Balkar A.S.S.R.

Resistance to the Soviet regime in the area is said to have gone on till 1923 when 'banditism' was liquidated.

Volume 31 of the first edition (1937) of the *Encyclopaedia* also has articles on the Karachai. The population of the Karachai Autonomous Province is given as 104,400 (1933), 81 per cent of it Karachai. On the history of the people it describes their conquest by Russia as 'one of the links in the colonial campaign of Tsarism in the Caucasus'. The Russian generals had announced in 1828 that 'the resistance of the Karachai is broken'. 'But', the article goes on to say, 'the struggle of the Karachai was not ended', for they participated in Shamil's Muridist movement against the Russians. Finally their resistance was suppressed and they were 'robbed' of their economic wealth. 'National oppression and ridicule by the Tsarist government made the difficult position of the Karachai twice as hard'. 'Several risings' took place, including trouble in 1873 and 1905. In 1917 the Karachai, for a time, lived in virtual independence. It is interesting to see how the article puts this. It says that it 'changed only the form of rule — instead of Tsarist agents — Atamans and Commissioners — the Karachai were governed by exploiters from the camp of bourgeois-nationalist elements'. This is a significant expression, applying as it would to any country setting itself up as independent under non-Communist rule.

The independence did not last. A detachment of the 9th Soviet Army entered the Karachai territory in August 1920 to 'give help' to such Communists as were in the area. 'The local counter-revolutionaries offered stubborn resistance. The struggle lasted one and a half months'. Later trouble was put down in 1920. The resistance of 'kulak' elements was broken in 1930 and, later in the thirties, 1,500 members of the Karachai Communist Party were purged as counter-revolutionary bourgeois elements. The history of the Karachai under Soviet rule is stated in the article's peroration to be 'a clear illustration of the attainments of Leninist-Stalinist national policy' and the Karachai themselves to be 'one of the leading members of the happy family of peoples of the U.S.S.R.'

Like the Chechens, they had their Soviet literature. The article on Karachai literature in Volume 31 (1937) mentions as one of its new classics a poem of praise called 'Stalin'.

Autonomous Republics and Provinces in the North Caucasus 1939, and the Limits of German Advance 1942.

Even after the war started the same line was maintained about the mountain peoples — right up to within months of the deportations, in fact. Kalinin, Chairman of the Presidium of the U.S.S.R. Supreme Soviet, declared in 1942:

> The Caucasus is the most enlightening demonstration of the reforming beneficial effect of the Soviet system on the psychology and character of people who, not without reason, saw danger to themselves everywhere. The Caucasians have now become a social people who see in the collective system their bulwark, the foundation of material prosperity and a higher intellectual life . . . the whole Caucasus has become one mountain village for its peoples. The whole Soviet land, from border to border, has

become their beloved home. (*Soviet War News*, October 6th, 1942.)

By October 5th, 1942, the Chechens had won 44 decorations in the Red Army — more than several much larger nations. Even in 1943 an official Soviet history mentioned as evidence of the unity of the Soviet peoples in the war the fact that in the period from December 9th, 1942, to March 31st, 1943, the Chechens and the Ingushi had contributed twelve million roubles, and the Kalmyks nine million roubles for the war effort. Seven and a half million roubles had also been contributed by the Kabardines and Balkars. (E. Genkina, *The Formation of the U.S.S.R.*, Moscow, 1943).

Thus, Soviet statements about the devotion and happiness of the Chechens and Ingushi, the Karachai and Balkars, were authoritative and repeated, throughout the peace and most of the war. After 1943 nothing seems to have been said about them, but this passed unnoticed among the eventful happenings of the end of the war, and it came as a surprise when a decree was published in *Izvestia* of June 26th, 1946, reading as follows:

Law concerning the Abolition of the Chechen-Ingush Autonomous Soviet Socialist Republic and the Changing of the Crimean Autonomous Soviet Socialist Republic into the Crimean Province.

During the Great Patriotic War, when the peoples of the U.S.S.R. were heroically defending the honour and independence of the Fatherland in the struggle against the German-Fascist invaders, many Chechens and Crimean Tatars, at the instigation of German agents, joined volunteer units organized by the Germans and, together with German troops, engaged in armed struggle against units of the Red Army; also at the bidding of the Germans they formed diversionary bands for the struggle against Soviet authority in the rear; meanwhile the main mass of the population of the Chechen-Ingush and Crimean A.S.S.R.s took no counter-action against these betrayers of the Fatherland.

In connection with this, the Chechens and the Crimean Tatars were resettled in other regions of the U.S.S.R., where they were given land, together with the necessary governmental assistance for their economic establishment. On the proposal of the Presidium of the Supreme Soviet of the R.S.F.S.R. the Chechen-Ingush A.S.S.R. was abolished and the Crimean A.S.S.R. was changed into the Crimean Province by decrees of the Presidium of the Supreme Soviet of the U.S.S.R.

The Supreme Soviet of the Russian Soviet Federative Socialist Republic resolves:

1. To confirm the abolition of Chechen-Ingush A.S.S.R. and the changing of the Crimean A.S.S.R. into the Crimean Province.

2. To make the necessary alterations and additions to Article 14 of the Constitution of the R.S.F.S.R.

Chairman of the Presidium of the Supreme Soviet of the R.S.F.S.R.,

I. Vlasov.

Secretary of the Presidium of the Supreme Soviet of the R.S.F.S.R.,

P. Bakhmurov.

Moscow, The Kremlin, 25th June, 1946.

It was later learnt that this deportation had taken place early in 1944. No statement of any sort about the Karachai and the Balkars was ever made. Their deportation was simply deduced indirectly in the circumstances narrated in Chapter 5.

D

Chapter 3

STEPPE, PENINSULA AND VOLGA

ON THE STEPPE: THE KALMYKS

A few hundred miles north of the well-watered and forest-covered highlands, where the egalitarian mountaineers fought for their natural rights, lived a very different people. The semi-desert steppe to the west of the Volga mouth has over its whole vast extent only a few areas, as in the Ergeni Hills, where cultivation is possible. In places great inland sand-dunes stretch for miles. The rainfall is only 4–8 inches a year. Dust storms are common.

There from the middle of the seventeenth century, a nation of tent-dwelling nomads, tending their sheep, cattle, horses and camels, lived under the rule of their Khan, appointed to reign over them by the living Buddha, the Dalai Lama in Lhasa himself. For the Kalmyks are Buddhists of the Zonkavist, or Lamaist, rite. They are also Mongols, not in some general sense, but literally: their language is virtually the same as that spoken in Mongolia proper. They used the old Mongol alphabet — indeed it was they who perfected it in 1646. Literary Mongolian was their written tongue until 1931.[1]

Soon after their arrival in the Volga area, as part of a migration from Chinese Turkestan, they became allies of the Russians, charged by Peter the Great with guarding the eastern frontier. This alliance gradually became vassalage. Finally, under Catherine the Great, they were deprived of their independence and in 1771 the Khanate was abolished.

Until that date their nation occupied, in addition to the

[1] W. K. Matthews, *Languages of the U.S.S.R.*, Cambridge, 1951.

36

area which later became the Kalmyk A.S.S.R. on the west bank of the Volga, an even larger territory on its eastern bank. In 1771 there occurred one of the most extraordinary events in any national history. A conspiracy was formed for escaping Russian oppression by a migration. It was designed that the entire nation should head eastwards until it was removed from the Russian yoke. It was only by accident that that section of the Kalmyks on the European side of the Volga was prevented from joining the larger portion of the population in this extraordinary move.

All this is mainly known to English readers through De Quincey's essay 'Revolt of the Tartars'. He says:

> There is no great event in modern history, or, perhaps it may be said more broadly, none in all history from its earliest records, less generally known, or more striking to the imagination, than the flight eastwards of a principal Tartar nation across the boundless steppes of Asia in the latter half of the last century.

As De Quincey says, it is remarkable as a conspiracy, as a great military expedition like that of Xenophon and as a great religious exodus — for one of the Kalmyk objections to Russian rule was its persecution of their Buddhist faith.

> Then, again, in the gloomy vengeance of Russia and her vast artillery, which hung upon the rear and the skirts of the fugitive vassals, we are reminded of Miltonic images.

In January 1771 representatives of the clans assembled and they were told by the organizers of the conspiracy

> of the oppressions of Russia; of her pride and haughty disdain evidenced towards them by a thousand acts; of her contempt for their religion; of her determination to reduce them to absolute slavery; of the preliminary measures she had already taken by erecting forts upon many of the great rivers in their neighbourhood; of the ulterior intentions she thus announced to circumscribe their pastoral lands, until they would all be obliged to renounce their flocks, and to collect in towns like Sarepta, there to pursue the mechanical and servile trades of shoe-maker, tailor and weaver, such as the free-born Tartar had always disdained.

De Quincey describes how for eight months, starting in the depths of winter, the entire nation fled, attacked at every step

by the Russians and their confederates, until they reached the
frontiers of China where the Emperor Kien Long received them
kindly and gave them land, and how he set a granite and brass
column to mark the occasion of their arrival telling how 'by
the favour of Kien Long, God's Lieutenant upon Earth, The
ancient Children of the Wilderness — the Torgote Tartars —
flying before the wrath of the Grecian Czar' found refuge.

An entire nation, amounting to 300,000 people with their
women and children had penetrated, with heavy loss, a distance
of 3,000 miles. If a few of De Quincey's details are inaccurate,
he conveys the feelings of the oppressed Kalmyks adequately.
Those who stayed behind faced the troubles their fellow-
nationals had fled to escape.

The Kalmyks remaining on the west bank of the Volga had
been confined to the bare stretch between the valleys of the
Volga and the Kuma. In this vast but sparsely settled area they
continued, until recently, their semi-nomadic herdsmen's life,
except for villages of fishermen on the low-lying Caspian coast.

It will not be worth repeating at much length for the
Kalmyks (or for the other nations dealt with) the examples of
the Soviet attitude given in the case of the Chechens. These are
much the same for each of them. But we may briefly look at
Volume 30 of the first edition of the *Large Soviet Encyclopaedia*
(1937). On the history of people it speaks of 'intensive colonial
robbery' by the Russians starting in 1668–71 and mentions
Kalmyk participation in the rebellion of 1707–8 and adds that
by the end of the eighteenth century Kalmykia was wholly a
colony of the Russian Empire.

Some light is thrown on the absence of class hatreds among
the Kalmyks by a description of their behaviour in 1905: 'The
Kalmyk peasantry, for the most part, showed itself the ideological prisoner of its own bourgeoisie, spiritual leaders and
feudalists'. For the aims of these undisputed leaders of the
Kalmyk people were national. They sought, the *Encyclopaedia*
says, autonomy, national representation in the Duma, irri-
gation, the right of Kalmyks to their own territory, and so on.

In 1917, too, Kalmyk revolutionary enthusiasm was of the

wrong sort and it had to be made up for by Russians: 'In 1917 the Astrakhan proletariat [i.e. *Russian* Bolsheviks] stood at the head of the revolution in the steppes'. At this time, in March 1917, a Kalmyk Congress set up a Central Committee with nationalist aims. After the revolution the Kalmyks carried out early in 1918 a 'counter-revolutionary rising against the Astrakhan workers'. A Kalmyk congress of Soviets could only be held in Astrakhan. Meanwhile the civil war raged on the Kalmyk steppe. On July 2nd, 1919, Lenin addressed a special letter to 'the toiling Kalmyk people'.

Part of Lenin's proclamation not quoted in the *Encyclopaedia*, runs:

> Your land has been seized by conquerors who are fighting to restore the rights of capitalists and landowners. They are helped by British and French capitalists who oppress hundreds of millions of your co-religionists in Asia.

In retrospect it is interesting to compare the present situation of the Buddhist inhabitants of Burma and Ceylon and of Kalmykia respectively. Lenin also added, 'Kalmyk brothers, the entire past of your people is an uninterrupted chain of suffering'.

In 1919 a decree was also issued forbidding further Russian settlement in Kalmyk lands (*Collection of Decrees and Regulations of the Workers' and Peasants' Government*, No. 37, Article 368). This, according to the *Encyclopaedia*, 'underlined the inviolability of Kalmyk territory'. It was followed by a political concession when in November 1920 a Kalmyk Autonomous Province was set up.

The *Encyclopaedia* article contains a number of other significant points. For instance it concedes that the Party organization in Kalmykia was only formed in 1918 and then had only 'a few members'. In 1921 the membership, including candidate members, was 609. Even in 1933 membership was only 3,143. In that year, however, the Autonomous Province became an Autonomous Soviet Socialist Republic. Kalmyk resistance had continued for a time. But 'banditism was finally liquidated in 1926'. And at the tenth Congress of the Kalmyk Soviets in 1931 it was proclaimed that 'stone by stone the indestructible foundation of the Kalmyk Socialist edifice is being laid'. During the war 20,000 Kalmyk soldiers were raised for the Red Army. Colonel Khomutnikov's Kalmyk Cavalry division was praised for special gallantry at Rostov in 1942. And in October 1942 a letter from the Kalmyks to Stalin on 'the determination of the Kalmyk people to mobilize all their resources to help the Red Army rout the invader' was much quoted.

The Kalmyks were still mentioned favourably even after the final withdrawal of the Germans from their territory in January 1943. The following month the Kalmyk Provincial Committee of the Communist Party announced various measures such as the re-opening of schools, and stated that the Kalmyks had collected seven million roubles for arms for the Red Army (*Soviet War News*, February 9th, 1943).

This was the last that was heard of them for fourteen years.

As in the case of the other deported peoples a Kalmyk pro-Soviet literature had been synthesized, and, as elsewhere, the older literature was ordered to be purged.

The genuine Kalmyk epic, *Dzhangar*, described by De Quincey as 'seventeen English miles in length', was found to be 'imbued with religious and reactionary content' and it was ordered 'to be carefully purged'. Meanwhile the heroes of the *Dzhangar* were transferred to a new epic *Yorel*, in which they assist Stalin to build 'the land of eternal youth, the land of abundance'. It concludes with an appeal to Stalin to 'lead us on to Communism' (*Poetry of Kalmykia*, Moscow, 1940).

The Kalmyks disappeared before the extremes of this method could be applied to their literature. An example of how it was performed in Stalin's later days, and in the time of his successors may be seen in the treatment of the Kirghiz epic, *Manas*.

> The expurgation of the epic should be strictly scientific and principled. It should take into account all the historical circumstances in the life of the people. This demands a suitable selection of variants, songs and episodes, a selection of which the fundamental principle must be the preservation in the epic of all the best elements inherent in the past of the Kirghiz people. (*Literaturnaya Gazeta*, May 27th, 1952.)

In *Sovetskaya Kirghizia* of March 23rd, 1956, there is a report of a meeting of the Department of Social Sciences of the Academy of Science of the Kirghiz S.S.R. on the new 'composite version' of the *Manas* epic. It stated that this epic had now been purged of mysticism, narrow nationalism, etc. There were complaints, however, that the idealization of the feudal past still seeped through, and further action was recommended. (Compare also *1984* by George Orwell, with its account of how it was necessary to 'produce garbled versions — definitive texts they were called' of poems which had become politically objectionable but which it was not wished to suppress entirely.)

The Kalmyks have often been treated, in spite of the distances and differences, as one of the nations of the Northern Caucasus. And, indeed, nothing separates their territory and Chechnia except the even more barren steppe between the Kuma and the Terek, inhabited yet more lightly by a few Nogai Tatars. Yet there are many differences: national, in that Kalmyks are Mongols; religious, in that they are Buddhist; historical, in their much earlier subjugation; geophysical and economic, in their steppe country and its livestock economy. And, again unlike the Chechens, during the war much of their territory, including the capital Elista, was occupied by the Germans, and a number of Kalmyks followed them in their retreat.

The deportation of the Kalmyks was the only one involving an entire republic of which no public statement was ever made. It was only indirectly that it was possible to deduce that they had followed their kinsfolk of the eighteenth century eastwards, without, however, finding a friendly reception at the end of the journey. The 'integrity of the Kalmyk territory' promised by Lenin, the 'indestructible edifice' which their republic had been asserted to be, did not stand the first strains put upon them.

IN THE PENINSULA: THE CRIMEAN TATARS

Unlike the little Caucasian peoples, content merely to defend the independence of their valleys and entering Russian history simply as the victims of distant campaigns of conquest and colonization, the Tatars of the Crimea had once formed a powerful and aggressive empire, often threatening Moscow itself.

The Tatars occupied the Crimea in the thirteenth century, at first forming an independent Khanate, but later coming under the suzerainty of the more powerful Turkish Empire. The relations between the two races were, and are, very near ones.

The Turkic languages are extremely close to one another. They can for most purposes be regarded as dialects of the same tongue — with negligible exceptions like Chuvash and Yakut. The Turkic peoples deported in 1943–4 are each closely affiliated in speech with other particular members of the Turkic family. The South Crimean Tatar dialect is closest to the Turkish of Turkey and to Turkmen. North Crimean and Karachai-Balkar are close to Kazakh and Kirghiz — though the Karachai and Balkar dialects have been influenced to some extent by their Caucasian neighbours (Balkar, for instance, having the 'th' sounds).

The Crimean Khanate itself, as a Mohammedan great power, warred with Poland, and with Russia too. It represents, in Russian literature, much of the grandeur of Oriental civilization at the time of its greatest confidence and strength. In Pushkin's *Fountain of Bakhchiserai*, the Khan Girei and his great palace are recreated for the imagination of Europe.

For many years, the area that is now the Ukraine was a practically empty buffer zone between the Khans and the Tsars. The frontier was gradually pushed south by settlements of Cossacks, and of foreign adventurers like those who temporarily formed the principality called 'Great Serbia'. And it was not until the early years of the eighteenth century that Peter the Great managed to annex Azov, on the Sea of Azov, thus for the first time reaching the southern waters. In 1711, however, his army and himself suffered disaster on the Pruth, and he was forced to retrocede the town. During the next half-century the various Turkish wars resulted in the establishment of Russian power on the Black Sea as well as the Sea of Azov. Finally the Crimea was isolated and invaded.

Full Russian annexation of the Crimea was preceded by the imposition in 1776 of a puppet, Khan Chagin Girei. This provoked a national rebellion in the following year which was put down by Russian troops at the beginning of 1778. The puppet Khan was again expelled by a rebellion in 1782. And in 1783, after Chagin Girei had again been restored by the Russian troops, he was forced to abdicate and the country was annexed to Russia.

During the following century a combination of deportation and emigration to Turkey reduced the Tatar population very considerably. They lost the best land and especially the fruitful coastal strip, concentrating in the mountains and the steppe. The Russian influx was considerable, and by the time of the revolution this once powerful nation had, like the Circassians, been reduced to numbers smaller even than those of the Chechens.

Earlier Soviet accounts of these and later events are, again, reasonably satisfactory. And, again, they rightly condemn certain Russian practices such as deportation.

Volume 35 of the first edition of the *Large Soviet Encyclopaedia* (1937) has an article on the 'Crimean A.S.S.R.' It describes the conquest of the area by the Tatars from previous nomads in the thirteenth century, their setting up of their own Khanate independent of the Golden Horde in 1425, with its capital at Bakhchisarai, and the influence on it of 'western Italian culture' from the Genoese settlements. After the fall of Constantinople the Khanate became in 1470 the vassal of Turkey. Russian attempts against it are described, including their first successful invasion in the war of 1736-9. The Turkish protectorate, the article says, long saved the Crimea from the Russians. In 1771 a new Russian invasion ended the Turkish connection. The Khanate was declared 'independent' with the Russians occupying certain forts. And in 1783 it was annexed to Russia. Land was given to palace favourites and 'heavy colonial oppression' caused mass emigration, so that 300,000 Tatars had gone by 1790. In the nineteenth century Russification and further 'dislodging' of the Tatars from the Crimea took place as a result of 'the anti-Tatar policy of the colonizers'.

In the autumn of 1854 there followed a decree of the Minister of War to the effect that 'the Emperor has ordered all inhabitants of the Muslim faith living in coastal areas to be removed from the coast into inland provinces'. This measure, which was carried out in connection with the Crimean War from considerations, as it were, of a military character, was needed by the Tsarist Government to enable it to seize the richest lands on the southern coast of the Crimea. The persecution and brutalities initiated against the Tatars by the military authorities because of their alleged acts of espionage, turned this transfer of population into a wholesale flight.

In 1860–2 231,177 Tatars emigrated, and Alexander II is condemned for approving this. Finally the Russian government, to prevent the whole area becoming a desert before Russians could be found to inhabit it, stopped further emigration. But a new wave of peasants who had been robbed of their land started to leave the country in the nineties. 'Inequality', 'national antagonism' and 'the moral and spiritual degradation of the oppressed people' are spoken of. And revolts, starting in 1808, are referred to.

In the nineteenth century Panturk feelings among the 'bourgeois intelligentsia' are mentioned, increasing greatly in the 1914 war when they became so widespread that 'the great influence of bourgeois nationalists among the broad Tatar masses contributed to the suppression of class contradictions'. In 1917 the 'nationalist-Tatar counter-revolution' with its party, the Milli Firka, took power, calling an all-Crimean Muslim Congress in Simferopol on March 25th. The main strength of the revolution in the Crimea is stated to have been the workers of Sebastopol, i.e. Russians. After the Bolshevik Revolution, the Tatar nationalists summoned a Kurultai in Bakhchisarai on September 10th, 1917, and set up a government with its own armed forces. Soviet power was established by Russian arms by February 1918, though it is admitted that 'the Crimean village' was not represented in the revolutionary committee.

Another Soviet account makes the role of Russian arms clearer still:

> Tatar bourgeois nationalists, having already united in the period of the February Revolution in the Milli Firka (national party), formed, in December 1917, their own 'national government' — the bourgeois nationalists' parliament (Kurultai) in Bakhchisarai. Here the struggle for the power of the Soviets was prolonged and bitter. The workers of Sevastopol and the revolutionary sailors of the Black Sea Fleet played a decisive role in this struggle. At the beginning of January 1918, the armies of the Kurultai were destroyed by revolutionary detachments and the power of the Soviets was established in Simferopol and, after Simferopol, throughout the Crimean Isthmus as well. (*Revolutsiya i Natsionalnosti*, No. 12, 1935, pp. 66–7.)

The *Encyclopaedia* goes on to speak of 'nationalist agitation' and kulak risings brought about by the Milli Firka. When the Germans approached the nationalists rose and again drove out the Communists. The German occupation, after a number of Soviet inroads, was followed by that of the White Army under Denikin which suppressed the nationalist 'directory'. In November 1920, the Soviets finally reconquered the country. And on October 18th, 1921, Lenin signed a decree setting up a Crimean A.S.S.R.

The *Encyclopaedia* goes on to say that the Milli Firka continued to resist, sowing 'national discord'. Nationalist feeling in the Communist party itself now became acute, as well as 'armed struggle in the form of banditism'. In 1928 the Central Committee liquidated 'Veli Ibrahimism', followers of the Crimean Communist President of the Republic, who was shot with many of his supporters about that time. There then took place the final 'uprooting of kulak-nationalist elements' from the Party. In 1936 the Party had 16,252 members of whom 2,257 were Tatars.

It is scarcely necessary to quote Soviet statements about the satisfactory position the Crimean Tatars had now attained. These resemble in every respect those made for all the other minorities of the U.S.S.R., and repeat almost word for word what has already been quoted about the Chechens. Their votes

in Soviet elections were adequately unanimous and the
speeches of their leaders full of loyalty and thanks to the
regime.

As for Crimean Tatar culture, the first edition of the *Large
Soviet Encyclopaedia* speaks of 'talented writers grown up in the
struggle with remnants of bourgeois nationalism'. But they
were in fact renowned for a lively folk literature, much of it
politically unobjectionable. As late as 1940 a Russian trans-
lation of some of these tales was produced in Moscow.

Their country was, unlike Checheno-Ingushetia, actually
occupied by the Germans. But reports continued to come out
about Tatar bravery in anti-German partisan units and in the
ranks of the Red Army. Some became Heroes of the Soviet
Union. So when the decree already quoted, on the dissolution
of the Chechen-Ingush and Crimean Republics, was published
in 1946, it was as much a surprise in the case of the Tatars as
in that of their Caucasian co-religionists.

On the Volga: The Germans

There have long been a number of Germans in Russia as
administrators, doctors and specialists in other fields in which
trained Russians were hard to come by in early Tsarist days.
But quite apart from these urbanized Germans there was a far
larger element — the peasant farmers. These started to come
to Russia on a big scale as a result of two decrees of Catherine
the Great in 1762 and 1763 calling for foreigners to settle the
empty lands from which the Russians had recently driven the
Khans. The Germans were extremely successful farmers. This
was partly due to their own qualities and partly to the fact that
they were almost the only free peasants in a country of serfs.
Though scattered to some extent over the whole arc of the
Russian south-east from the Ukraine to the Urals their great
centre was in the area later to become the Volga-German
A.S.S.R.

Volume 41 of the first edition of the *Large Soviet Encyclopaedia*
(1939 — i.e. only two years before the suppression of the
republic) has an article on the Volga-German A.S.S.R. It

quotes the decrees of Catherine the Great which invited the
Germans in and the privileges, such as exemption from military
service granted them as an incentive. It adds that in the 1880's
they 'lost their privileges, suffered Russification' and under-
went other oppressions. The bourgeoisie, it is stated, got control
of 36·5 per cent of their land — a smaller proportion than that
later acquired by the Soviet government. The German
peasants, who had taken part in the Pugachev revolt in the
eighteenth century, also revolted in 1905.

In 1916 there was promulgated a law against 'German
dominance', the application of which was also extended to cover
the Volga Germans. Shortly after this preparations were put in
hand for the expulsion of all Germans from the Volga area, and
this was set for April 1917. The overthrow of the monarchy
prevented the carrying out of this barbarous measure. When
the colonists appealed to the Provisional Government to revoke
this law, Kerensky only agreed 'to stay the execution of the
decree'. Only the Great October Socialist Revolution, which
put an end to national oppression . . . rescinded this decree.

The article goes on to say that in February 1917 the 'bourgeoisie and kulaks' of the area came to power, and that they
tried to maintain an Autonomous German Province. After the
October Revolution, Stalin set up a Commissariat for Volga-
German Affairs and, after the defeat of an anti-Soviet rising,
Lenin, on October 19th, 1918, decreed the setting up of an
autonomous administration —though not on the terms asked for
by the local nationalists. Several German units are named by
the article as having taken part in the Civil War on the Red
side. The purges of the late twenties and early thirties are
referred to as 'a struggle with nationalist tendencies' and it is
added that the Central Committee of the All-Union-
Communist Party 'and the healthy core of the Party organization of the Volga Germans made it possible to defeat the
nationalist-kulak tendency'. This is one of the most direct
references in the articles we are considering, to the fact that
even a section of a local Party—that not included in 'the healthy
core' — was 'nationalist' (i.e. opposed to Moscow domination)
and pro-'kulak' (i.e. opposed to oppression of the peasantry

and collectivization). It seems not unreasonable to assume that the non-Communist sections of the population were even more affected by these heresies.

The article adds that as a result of the 'carrying out of Leninist-Stalinist national policy' the area 'became a republic of flourishing socialist culture', and stresses the loyalty of the Germans equally with their prosperity in such passages as:

> During the first and second Stalin Five-Year Plans, in the periods of the all-out Socialist offensive against the capitalist elements of town and country, the Volga-German Autonomous Soviet Socialist Republic was the foremost in carrying out collectivization in the countryside, and effectively mechanized its agriculture. Industry also developed . . . The future development of the national economy and culture of the Volga-German Autonomous Soviet Socialist Republic, its rapid progress towards a better, still more joyous life, and towards Communism, are guaranteed by the Stalinist Constitution, by the resolute Stalinist leadership of the Central Committee of the Bolshevik Communist Party of the Soviet Union and the limitless devotion of the working people of the Volga-German Autonomous Soviet Socialist Republic to the cause of Communism.

The Volga Germans were one of the very first Soviet peoples to gain a form of autonomy in the 'German Volga Labour Commune' proclaimed in October 1918 and given the status of Autonomous Soviet Socialist Republic in February 1924. The area in 1926 had 66·4 per cent Germans in its population as against 20·4 per cent Russians and 12 per cent Ukrainians. And (a characteristic usual in Russian dependent territories though perhaps unexpected in connection with Germans) the local people formed the peasantry and the main urban population was Russian. The effect of this became even more pronounced when the capital was moved from the old German centre, Marxstadt to the Russian town of Pokrovsk (renamed Engels) in August 1922. 86 per cent of the population of the town were then Russians and Ukrainians and only 11 per cent Germans.

The collectivization campaign and the great purges hit the Volga German Republic as hard, though perhaps no harder, than it did other areas. The Prime Minister, Welsch, who had attacked 'nationalist and other anti-Soviet elements' in the Government and Party of the Republic in 1936, was himself arrested in 1937 together with other high officials including the President of the Republic.

After collectivization the Volga German farms were, as we have seen, given special praise. The Soviet English daily *Moscow News* said on January 16th, 1939, 'These people are demonstrating to the whole world what the industrious gifted German people are capable of when they are free from the yoke of capitalism'. And in general the Volga Republic was treated as somewhat of a show place.

On June 26th, 1938, in the elections in the Volga German A.S.S.R. 99·7 per cent of the votes were cast for the official candidates.

The deportation of the Volga Germans was an announcement of the failure of Soviet policy in the face of the ties of nationality. Nevertheless it was regarded at the time as an exceptional case. The decree, which came in September 1941, was couched in the following terms:

According to trustworthy information received by the military authorities there are among the German population living in the Volga area thousands and tens of thousands of diversionists and spies who on a signal being given from Germany are to carry out sabotage in the area inhabited by the Germans of the Volga.

None of the Germans living in the Volga area have reported to the Soviet authorities the existence of such a large number of diversionists and spies among the Volga Germans; consequently the German population of the Volga area conceals enemies of the Soviet people and of Soviet authority in its midst.

In case of diversionist acts being carried out at a signal from Germany by German diversionists and spies in the Volga German Republic or in the adjacent areas and bloodshed taking place, the Soviet Government will be obliged, according to the laws in force during the war period, to take punitive measures against the whole of the German population of the Volga.

In order to avoid undesirable events of this nature and to prevent serious bloodshed, the Presidium of the Supreme Soviet of the U.S.S.R. have found it necessary to transfer the whole of the German population living in the Volga area into other areas, with the promise, however, that the migrants shall be allotted land and that they should be given assistance by the State in settling in the new areas.

For the purpose of resettlement, areas having much arable land in the Novosibirsk and Omsk provinces, the Altai territory, Kazakhstan and other neighbouring localities have been allotted.

In connexion herewith the State Committee of Defence has been instructed to carry out urgently the transfer of all Germans of the Volga and to allot to the Germans of the Volga who are being transferred lands and domains in the new areas.

President of the Presidium of the Supreme Soviet of the U.S.S.R.:

(Signed)   M. KALININ.

Secretary of the Presidium of the Supreme Soviet of the U.S.S.R.:

(Signed)   A. GORKIN.

Moscow: Kremlin, August 28, 1941.

(Bulletin of the Supreme Soviet of the U.S.S.R.,
No. 38, September 2nd, 1941.)

A later decree (of September 7th, 1941) divided the Volga German territory — fifteen regions going to the Saratov and seven to the Stalingrad provinces. *(Bulletin of the Supreme Soviet,* No. 40 (1941): quoted in *Collection of Laws of the Soviet Union and Decrees of the Presidium of the Supreme Soviet 1938–1958,* Moscow, 1958.)

Thus a people whose 'devotion to Communism' had been publicly asserted and who had demonstrated their unanimity in Soviet elections were submitted to a fate officially described as 'barbarous' when threatened by the Tsars.

Chapter 4

HOW MANY WENT?

The total numbers deported in these operations can only be estimated, for a variety of reasons. A basic figure can, indeed, be obtained easily enough. The Soviet census of 1939 gives the following figures:

Chechens	407,690
Ingushi	92,074
Karachai	75,737
Balkars	42,666
Kalmyks	134,271

The Volga Germans and Crimean Tatars are not listed. But the *Large Soviet Encyclopaedia* gives them as percentages of the population of their A.S.S.R.s, as follows:

Volga Germans
66·4% of
576,000 - 382,000 (1933)
(*L.S.E.*, Vol. 41,
1st edition)

This is kept in round numbers as the original is a Soviet estimate in round numbers, not a census figure.
(The total population of the Republic in 1939 was 605,542.)

Crimean Tatars
23·1% of
875,100 - 202,000 (1936)
(*L.S.E.*, Vol. 35,
1st edition)

(The total population was 1,126,824 in 1939 which implies that the 1936 estimate is low.)

Total - 1,336,438

Even assuming that the census was accurate and that the estimates on the Germans and Tatars are sound, this is plainly not an entirely satisfactory figure. In the first place, other Soviet *estimates* were often significantly different from the figures produced in 1939. For instance the 1933 estimate of Karachai gives *c.* 84,800, as against the census figure of 75,737; while the Ingush estimate in 1937 is 82,000, as against 92,074 in the census. On the other hand the Kalmyk 1937 estimate is 129,800, which is close, and the Balkars, 41,000 in 1935, is closer still. The Crimean figure appears the most dubious, and may require inflation by up to thirty or forty thousand. The Germans would perhaps have increased by *c.* 20,000. This would give just under 1,400,000.

Another slightly dubious method, which has been used, is to apply to the latest pre-war population estimates of republics etc. (1941) the percentages of autochthons given in the 1926 census, whose figures are reliable. This ignores fifteen years in which the proportion of Russians has certainly increased, and results in an estimate nearly fifty thousand higher than we have given. If we correct it with reasonable assumptions about the Russian influx, especially in the case of Chechnia, we reduce it to a figure of just over 1,300,000. This accords reasonably with the more direct method, differing from it in principle only in that it omits members of the races not inhabiting their national territory.

The 1939 census was suspect for a number of reasons. But there is no particular suspicion attached to its figures on the populations listed here, and since they check rather well with other approaches, we may accept them as reasonable. They are in any case the official figures.

Our official figure of *c.* 1,336,000 does not allow for the natural increase of population from 1939, 1936 and 1933 in the various cases. But nor does it allow for the losses incurred during the actual progress of the war. These were presumably negligible for the Volga Germans, and comparatively small for the Chechens, whose territory the Germans barely reached. But the Kalmyks, and still more the Crimean Tatars may have lost considerably, mainly in the course of partisan action against the returning Soviet forces, and the reprisals following this (the numbers who accompanied the German retreat seem to have been only a few thousand). And the initial Soviet penal measures, though involving a good number of executions, consisted largely of the arrest and despatch of recalcitrants to labour camps. We may perhaps reckon these deportees as high as fifty thousand in all the area concerned. But, though they did not figure in the greater mass actions that followed, it does not seem unreasonable to count them as having undergone the same fate and not alter our statistics to exclude them.

If the losses of the war make the 1,336,000 an overestimate, there are countervailing considerations. The total number of Germans in the U.S.S.R. was 1,423,000 on the eve of the war. Some of them were in Soviet Asian settlements already, but those in the European parts of the U.S.S.R. were deported together with their fellow nationals in the Volga, and their various National Districts were abolished in the same way as the Volga Republic. It is difficult to estimate the numbers involved, for most of these Districts were in the Ukraine, and many were overrun by the Nazis before the Soviet authorities could take action. On their withdrawal the Nazis evacuated all Germans. It has been estimated that the Russians succeeded in deporting about 200,000 from the Ukraine, the Crimea and the North Caucasus (Kolarz, op. cit., p. 75), and we may conservatively reckon the same number again from other parts of Russia. And we might perhaps treat them as a numerical imponderable which in any case very much outweighs any conceivable losses in population of the deported nations during the war.

These non-Volga Germans are, however, not strictly speaking my concern in this book, any more than the million odd Balts and the similar number of Ukrainian deportees who followed them.

So, leaving them aside, and assuming improbably heavy war losses, we get the following result:

	assumed percentage loss	assumed loss
Crimean Tatars - - -	20%	c. 40,000
Kalmyks - - - -	10%	c. 13,000
Chechens and Ingushi - -	5%	c. 25,000
Karachai and Balkars - -	5%	c. 6,000
	Total:	84,000

If we subtract this from our original 1,336,438 we are left with a figure of just over 1,250,000. This round number, of a million and a quarter souls, may perhaps be taken as a reckoning, conservative enough to be acceptable to everybody, of those despatched into exile in General Serov's cattle-trucks in a particular set of deportation operations distinguished from others of the sort in a single respect — that this time it was whole peoples that were being sent into oblivion.

The size of the depopulated territories was approximately 60,000 square miles. That is, seventeen times the area of the island of Cyprus; or the size of Czechoslovakia and Albania together.

It was divided as follows:

Chechen-Ingush A.S.S.R. - - - -	6,060
Crimean A.S.S.R. - - - - -	10,036
Kabardine-Balkar A.S.S.R.: estimate of Balkar area - - - - - - -	950
(Total 4,747)	
Kalmyk A.S.S.R. - - - - - -	28,641
Volga German A.S.S.R. - - - -	10,503
Karachai A.P. - - - - - -	3,831
	60,011

European settlers, mainly Russian, took the land.

Chapter 5

BEHIND THE SOVIET SILENCE

———◦◦◦◦———

In this chapter we examine Soviet publications for information about the deportations and deported nations. The results are extraordinary, not to say sinister, by the standards prevailing in the non-Communist world. Direct information about anything involved — even the past existence of these peoples — was, in fact, almost totally suppressed. Inspection of Soviet documents rapidly becomes a piece of detective work, a search for indirect clues, rather than normal reference activity.

With very few exceptions, which we will deal with, nothing was said about the nations concerned for a period of about ten years. Apart from the Chechen-Ingush and Crimean decree published in *Izvestia* in June 1946, they seem simply to have disappeared from the category of admitted entities. They are ignored almost as if they had never been — in some cases, exactly as if they had never been. There are precedents for this occurring in the case of individuals in the U.S.S.R.: men like Kossior and Eikhe, or Meyerhold and Babel, were for decades what George Orwell christened 'unpersons'. The 'unnation' was a new phenomenon.

When the decree on the suppression of the Chechen-Ingush and Crimean Republics became known in 1946, and those interested began to examine the maps which then appeared giving the new territorial arrangements, they noticed that certain other national areas had disappeared too. Moreover, as Mr. Kolarz points out (*Russia and her Colonies*, p. 75), if simple transfer of population had been all that was implied, 'it would have been conceivable for the Volga German republic to be resurrected on the banks of the Ob, Irtysh or Yenesei', and similarly with the other nations. No such republics were shown.

What the maps did show was that the Volga German, Chechen-Ingush, Crimean and Kalmyk republics and the Karachai Autonomous Province had disappeared, and that the Kabardine-Balkar republic now existed only in truncated form as the Kabardine A.S.S.R. simply. Except for the Crimea, which now appeared as the Crimean Province, the missing autonomous units had all been partitioned:

The Volga German A.S.S.R. went mainly to the Saratov Province, with the southern strip going to the Stalingrad Province.

The Kalmyk A.S.S.R. was mainly incorporated in a new Astrakhan Province, with smaller areas handed over to the Stalingrad Province, the Rostov Province and the Stavropol Territory.

The Karachai Autonomous Province was largely ceded to the Georgian S.S.R., with smaller areas going to the Krasnodar Territory, the Cherkess Autonomous Province and the Stavropol Territory.

The Upper Baksan Valley, the main Balkar area, went to Georgia, while the rest of Balkaria remained in the newly renamed Kabardine A.S.S.R.

The Chechen-Ingush A.S.S.R. was mainly incorporated in a new Grozny Province, with a western strip consisting of most of Ingushetia going to the North Ossetian A.S.S.R., an eastern area, with Shamil's old capital Vedeno, handed over to the Daghestan A.S.S.R., and the mountainous southern portion ceded to the Georgian S.S.R.

In most cases, as we shall see, the place names in the old local languages had also gone, being replaced by new Russian ones.

The deduction from this, and other material we will consider later, was that the Kalmyks, Karachai and Balkars had been deported too. This was true, but it was to receive no official confirmation until 1957.

A look at the political and physical map shows that in the case of the Karachai, Balkars, Ingushi and Chechens the territorial rearrangements were rather peculiar. As we have said, the main Karachai and Balkar regions to the north and east of Mount Elbruz respectively were both annexed to Georgia which also obtained a large area of the south part of the former Chechen-Ingush Republic. An important gain was also made by the North Ossetian Autonomous Republic.

Administrative Divisions in the North Caucasus 1945

This provides some insight into the rating of the nations by the Soviet government. Georgia, Stalin's (and Beria's) home republic, was inordinately favoured. Moreover its spread right across the dividing line of the main chain of the Caucasus was unprecedented. In fact the division of the Ossetian nation into two separate administrative areas — the North Ossetian A.S.S.R. and the South Ossetian Autonomous Province (the latter forming part of Georgia) had been justified on the grounds of the physical division produced by the mountains.

That the North Ossetian Republic was given an increase in

territory over an area hitherto unconnected with it, while the
Kabardines were only allotted part of the Balkar area previously
administered from their own capital, Nalchik, also tends to
confirm that the Kabardines were at this time less well thought
of than the Ossetians. It is perhaps relevant that the Central
Committee decree of February 10th, 1948, criticizing Muradeli's opera *The Great Friendship*, while condemning the
Chechens and Ingushi for their actions in the 1917 Revolution
finds it necessary to put forward the Ossetians and Georgians
only as reputable nations.

It was with interest that new editions of other Soviet
reference books were looked at, for what further information
they might now give about the deported nations. It was found
that they now said — nothing at all. Not only was each
nation's present obliterated, but its past as well. Except in very
occasional circumstances their names had become almost
literally unspeakable. This silence, only practicable in a land
with a totalitarian state organization, was a strong indication
of the regime's view of truth. It also gave little reason to suppose
that the Chechens, the Kalmyks and the others were likely to
be receiving good treatment.

The sources that can be checked for such negative evidence
are plainly of rather a special nature. If there happened to be
no book published or article written in Britain for a number of
years about, say, British Somaliland, it might be odd, but
would scarcely prove anything. But there are certain publications which must ordinarily deal with all areas and peoples
and from which their omission is significant. In the first place
compilations such as encyclopaedias come to mind. And a good
deal of the most striking information comes from the second
edition of the *Large Soviet Encyclopaedia*.

This important orthodox and official compilation has so far
had two editions. The volumes appear (apart from certain
irregularities) one by one in alphabetical order. The last
volume of the first edition came out in 1948. The second
edition, in larger volumes, then started to come out in 1949 and
was completed, with its fifty-first volume, in 1958.

Before we look at the second edition of the *Encyclopaedia* we can refer to the last volumes of the first edition which came out after the deportations. There are only a few of them, one being Volume 50, which has an article on the North Ossetian Autonomous Republic. It appeared in September 1944, and showed on the accompanying sketch map that the republic was bounded by the Kabardine Republic — not the Kabardine-Balkar Republic — and the Grozny Province — not the Chechen-Ingush Republic. It seems that no-one noticed this at the time. And in the same volume it was found possible to assert, in a short article on the North Caucasus, that in the war 'The mountain nationalities of the North Caucasus had displayed outstanding heroism both in the Red Army and in extensive partisan fighting'.

The composite volume of the first edition on *The U.S.S.R.* came out in October 1947. The names of the abolished republics and deported peoples are not given either in lists or on maps. On p. 60 the population of the U.S.S.R. is listed by 'national composition', within the 1939 boundaries. The 20,000 Assyrians are listed. 88,000 Adygei and 164,000 Kabardines are noted. The number of Greeks in the U.S.S.R. is given as 285,900. But none of the then deported nations is named, unless indeed they are under 'others' of whom there are 2,983,000. The only oblique hint at a missing people, the Balkars, is given in the population of the Kabardine Republic as of 1933, which is said to have been 60 per cent Kabardine and 10·7 per cent Russian, simply.

We have already quoted largely from the first edition, and it will now be seen how useful a comparison has thus been provided with what was not given in the second edition. For the existence of the first edition provides a way of checking the sort of space and treatment given to a nation or area in the ordinary way — a control, as the scientists say.

The new edition is most attractively produced and the scientific and certain other articles are very well done. It is a thorough publication, and is printed in 300,000 copies. The importance attached to it by the Soviet authorities, as an

expression of right-mindedness, is very great, as various recent
incidents show. The fact that the volume containing the article
on Stalin, No. 40, was delayed for over a year, until every other
succeeding volume had already been produced, shows that
decisions on these matters are not made lightly nor on a low
level. In two cases in the last five years special measures of a
rather startling kind have been taken: the sending round to
subscribers of instructions to remove certain pages and replace
them with others supplied. The first dealt with the excision of
a long article on Beria and its replacement by photographs of
the Bering Sea and an article on an eighteenth-century figure
called Berggolz, and the second, similarly, ordered the removal
of the article on the purged Chinese Communist leader, Kao
Kang (Gao Gang in Russian) and its replacement by articles
on various towns in Africa and elsewhere beginning with the
relevant letter.

It will be seen from the dates that the greater bulk of the
second edition of the *Encyclopaedia* had come out before there
was any question of the 1957 rehabilitations of deported nations,
but that some of the later volumes followed that announcement:
thus the treatment of Balkars, Kalmyks or Ingushi might be
expected to be different from that of Chechens — Ch being a
late letter in the Russian alphabet.

As we shall see, the first slight signs of any recognition of the
existence of the deported peoples began to appear in 1955. But
the first fairly definite indication that restoration was intended
for the majority of them came in Khrushchev's Secret Speech.
This was made in February 1956. The last volume to come out
before that speech was Volume 38, taking things as far as
SIG.

By this time the bulk of the deportees and their areas could
have been covered. The Balkars, Karachai, Kalmyks and
Ingushi, as races, and the Germans too; the Karachai Autonomous Province, the Kalmyk Autonomous Soviet Socialist
Republic, the Kabardine-Balkar Autonomous Soviet Socialist
Republic, the Crimean Autonomous Soviet Socialist Republic,
the Volga German Autonomous Soviet Socialist Republic, as

political units; and the Caucasus as a historical and ethnic area of study, should have had individual articles, as in the first edition, giving some information about the nations.

The second edition contains no articles at all on the Balkars, the Ingushi, the Kalmyks, the Kalmyk A.S.S.R., the Karachai, the Karachai Autonomous Province or the Volga German Republic.

Instead of an article on the Kabardine Balkar A.S.S.R., there is one on the Kabardine A.S.S.R. (in Volume 19). It runs to thirteen and a half pages. There is no mention of the Balkars. The population is said to be mainly Kabardine, with 40 per cent Russian and Ukrainian. A misrepresentation of the facts occurs, as the republic is referred to as simply 'Kabardine' at the time of its foundation in 1936 and in the settling of its constitution in the following year, whereas it was then actually called 'Kabardine-Balkar'. The authors do not find it out of place to add that 'the Tsarist government and local feudalists artificially aroused national enmity between the mountaineers and differences between the mountaineers and the Russian Cossacks'. Nor do they fail to conclude:

> Right from the time of the setting up of the Soviet power the peoples of Kabarda, thanks to the putting into practice of Leninist-Stalinist national policy, received every opportunity for political economic and cultural development, in brotherly comradeship with the other nations of the U.S.S.R. . . .

The article on 'Germans' in Volume 29 (November 1954) speaks of the Germans outside Germany as existing in 'Southern Denmark, Eastern Belgium, the U.S.A., Canada, Brazil, the Argentine and Roumania'. (It adds that by decision of the Potsdam Conference about ten million Germans were transferred to Germany from the territories of Poland, Czechoslovakia and Hungary.) Thus, though the small numbers of Germans in such countries as Brazil and Canada are mentioned, there is nothing at all on the Volga and other Germans of the U.S.S.R. (who are not referred to throughout the article).

Volume 23 has an article on the Crimean Province — founded, it states, on June 30th, 1944. The basic population is

given as Russian and Ukrainian, and it is mentioned that there
have been immigrants from the Russian provinces of Kursk,
Penza, Rostov and elsewhere. There is nothing about the
previously existing republic. But the Crimean past is so very
important in Russian history, that it seems to have not been
feasible to eliminate it entirely. And Volume 23 also has an
article on the Crimean Khanate which, unlike the attitude of
the first edition, is treated in an extremely hostile fashion, as a
centre of the slave trade and aggression in general. 'In the
seventeenth century the Russian government began to prepare
the annihilation of the robber Crimean Khanate'. The annexation of the area, at a time when it was supposed to be independent, is justified because anti-Russian elements are said to have
wished to return to the Turkish connection. 'The unification of
the Crimean Khanate to Russia in 1783 had great progressive
significance in the history of the peoples of the Crimea and led
to the liquidation of Turkish-Tatar aggression in the Crimea.'
It also 'had great progressive significance for the social
economic and cultural development of the Crimea'.

After the annexation the Tatars are not mentioned again
until the time of the revolution, when they are referred to three
times: first in connection with 'stubborn resistance to the Soviet
power shown by the Panturk leaders of Tatar bourgeois
nationalism', secondly in that Tatar nationalists treacherously
captured and shot Bolsheviks, and thirdly when 'the Germans
set up a cruel colonial regime assisted by the Tatar nationalists'.

A comparison of the maps in the article on the Crimean
A.S.S.R. in the first edition of the *Encyclopaedia* with those on
the Crimean Province in the second edition shows a number of
changes of name and the disappearance of many, though not
all, of those in Tatar. For example Buyuk-Orlar becomes
Oktyabrskoye (October). (The later map was prepared in
November 1952.)

In Volume 19 the article on the Caucasus has three pages
on 'ethnic composition' which deals in addition with the
autonomous republics and provinces of the area, by which,
'nations of a new type — socialist — were set up'. There is no

reference to the deported peoples or their former administrative areas.

In the article in the same volume on the Caucasian Wars
Chechnia, though not the Chechens as such, is mentioned
twice — once on a historical map and once in the following
sentence: 'England activized the activity of her agents among
the Caucasian mountaineers, as a result of which there was a
new outburst of the Muridist movement, especially in Chechnia
and Daghestan'.

It might perhaps have been expected that reference, if only
historical, would be made to the deported peoples in the
articles on the Russian provinces in which their homelands
were now included.

The provinces and territories concerned were those of
Astrakhan, Grozny, Krasnodar, Saratov, Stavropol and
Stalingrad. The last two came out after the rehabilitations and,
showing different circumstances, are dealt with in Chapter 13
(though it may be noted that even then the Stalingrad article
contains no reference to its former Germans, who had not been
rehabilitated).

In Volume 3 (May 1950) there is an article on the Astrakhan
Province into which the accompanying map shows the greater
part of the Kalmyk A.S.S.R. to have been incorporated. In this
seven and a half page article there is no reference, historically
or otherwise, to the Kalmyks. It is stated that besides population
increases in the town, 'in the years of Soviet power the population has grown also in the rest of the Astrakhan Province — in
the semi-desert steppe'. It is also stated that the 'majority of
the population of the Astrakhan Province is Russian. The
Kazakhs, Tatars and Ukrainians form significant groups.' The
only hint of the past occurs when it is stated that there are two
towns in the province — Astrakhan and 'Stepnoi (formerly
Elista)'. Apart from Elista itself many of the village names
which in the map in the first edition are of Mongol character
such as Ulan-Erge, Yusta and so on are here changed to
Russian ones like Krasnoi ('Red') and Trudovoi ('Labour').
Stepnoi, the new name of the capital, was Russian, and

similarly the main fishing settlement Lagan turns to Kaspiiski. The article also mentions that the Astrakhan Province was set up on December 27th, 1943. This fits with early unofficial statements that the Kalmyk A.S.S.R. was dissolved by a decree given that date, and published in the republic at the time of the deportation.

Similarly the article on the Grozny Province (Volume 13, June 1952) contains no reference, historical or otherwise, to the Chechens and Ingushi. Names on the map have become mainly Russianized — Krasnoarmeiskoye, Sovietskoye, Mezhdurechiye, etc. The province's date of formation is given as March 22nd, 1944, but, as we shall see later, it was not formed directly on the dissolution of the Chechen A.S.S.R.

The Krasnodar Territory (Volume 23, October 1953) is shown as having annexed the upper Laba Valley from the former Karachai Autonomous Province. The population of the territory as listed includes no Karachai.

The article on the Saratov Province (Volume 38, December 1955) has no reference to Germans. The basic population is given as Russian with Ukrainian, Chuvash, Mordvin and Tatar minorities. A map shows that all the place names are now Russian, with the doubtful concession of Engels: Marxstadt becomes plain Marx.

And similarly with the articles on Georgia and North Ossetia, which had obtained parts of the suppressed autonomous territories.

Though virtually nothing thus emerges in the way of references to the deported peoples in the new accounts of their home territories, it seemed possible that they would now be dealt with in the articles on the areas to which they were deported.

In the case of the Germans, these had been officially stated to include 'the Novosibirsk and Omsk Provinces, the Altai Territory and Kazakhstan'.

The article on Novosibirsk Province in Volume 30 (December 1954) states: 'The predominant masses of the population consist of Russians' and it names 'Ukrainians and Tatars', comprising an 'insignificant percentage of the population'. The article on the Omsk Province in Volume 31 (February 1955) says 'The basic part of the population is Russian; it is inhabited also by Ukrainians, Kazakhs, Tatars and others'.

The Altai Territory article in Volume 2 (March 1950) says that 'The predominant mass of the population' is Russian, the next in number Ukrainians, and 'in no great number Chuvashes and Kazakhs', and 'in the High-Altai Autonomous Province the basic population consists of Altais'. The article on the High-Altai Autonomous Province in Volume 12 (May 1952) speaks simply of a basic population of Russians and Altais.

It was later made clear that not only Germans, but also a number of the other deported nationalities had been sent to Kazakhstan and Kirghizia. For instance (see p. 130) Chechen and Ingush newspapers began to appear in these territories in 1955–6. However the articles on the Kazakh and Kirghiz S.S.R.s in the second edition of the *Large Soviet Encyclopaedia* make no references to these peoples. In Volume 19, passed for publication on June 16th, 1953, the article on Kazakhstan says 'the basic population is Kazakh, forming with Russians 80 per cent of the whole population of the republic. In Kazakhstan are also settled Ukrainians, Uzbeks, Uigurs, Dungans, Tatars, Koreans [!], Karakalpaks, etc'. The Kazakhs, it adds, live 'in close comradeship with the Russian, Ukrainian and other bordering nations'. Similarly in Volume 21, passed for publication on June 13th, 1953, the article on Kirghizia mentions among the population the Kirghiz and eight other peoples among whom the deported ones are not named. Here too there is a reference to 'mutual trust' which prevails as a result of 'Leninist-Stalinist national policy'.

The *Encyclopaedia* shows it most bluntly. But the same nil return was made by other reference books of similar type. A few examples will show the essence of what was an almost universal phenomenon.

Economic Geography of the U.S.S.R., by N. N. Baranski (for the eighth class in Middle Schools), Moscow, 1949, states that in national composition the North Caucasus is very varied. Among the basic population living here before the arrival of the Russians several tens of various nationalities may be reckoned. In their great majority they are united in autonomous republics and autonomous provinces.

It goes on to name those of the Adygei, the Cherkess, the Kabardines, the Ossetians and the Daghestanis, but no others, of those living there in pre-Russian times.

The *Soviet Atlas* No. IV for Middle Schools (On the History of the Soviet Union) falsifies the position, in that it leaves out of its map of the administrative divisions of the Soviet Union in 1922 all the territories which were *later* suppressed. The Crimean Republic, for instance, had been founded in 1921, but is not shown.

A Geography of the U.S.S.R. by N. I. Lyalikov (Moscow, 1955), described as for teachers, has in its chapter on the Caucasus a section on 'population' in which the offending nations are not mentioned even historically. The Tsarist campaigns are said to have been against simply 'the mountaineers'. 'Bourgeois-nationalism' during the Civil War is referred to. And non-deported races like the Kabardines, Circassians and the Ossetians are listed. In the section on national autonomy the republics and areas listed do not include those suppressed earlier. Such was the general run of things.

The constitutional formalities were observed in the February 1947 session of the Supreme Soviet of the U.S.S.R., when, on the basis of a speech by Vyshinsky, Article 22 of the Constitution was amended to list the administrative divisions of the country, omitting the suppressed republics. The earlier text was not referred to.

There was a further unmistakable indication that the deportees had lost all civil rights. Not only were no new autonomous regions erected for them, but their previous representation in the Soviet of Nationalities of the Supreme Soviet, which supposedly guards the interests of the minorities, was suppressed. *Izvestia* of June 15th, 1950, lists the nationalities represented there after the 1950 elections. There are none from the nations in question. In the Soviet of Nationalities elected in 1937 they had the following numbers: Volga Germans 10; Kalmyks 9; Chechens 5; Balkars 4; Karachai 3; Ingushi 1. (The Crimean representation was not clearly differentiated, but seems to have been 5 or 6.)

The administrative reference books, like the maps, showed the new territorial arrangements.

Already, the 1942 edition of the Soviet handbook on *Administrative Divisions of the R.S.F.S.R.* has, in its section on administrative changes, in the pages dealing with the Saratov province, a list renaming former areas of the Volga German Republic now incorporated in that province: for example Neu-Wolte has become Sverdlovo. A decree of the U.S.S.R., and three decrees of the R.S.F.S.R. are referred to as authority for the changes.

Similarly, the 1954 edition[1] of the handbook *U.S.S.R.: Territorial Administrative Divisions of the Union Republics* gives the whole new layout formally, together with a list of changes of name, most of them unconnected with our subject, but a fair number being Russifications of Chechen, Tatar and Kalmyk place names. It shows Northern Ossetia increased in area from 6·2 thousand square kilometres to 9·2; Daghestan from 35·0 to 38·2, and Georgia from 69·3 to 76·4.

Changes of name are also referred to in, for example, a decree of the Presidium of the Supreme Soviet of the U.S.S.R., published on February 1st, 1952, renaming twenty-nine railway stations in the Crimean Province. Russian names are substituted for the Tatar names, e.g. Taganash becomes Solenoye Ozero, Karankut becomes Otradnaya, and so on. These alterations of place-name in the Crimea continued after the Province was transferred, by a Decree of the Supreme Soviet of February 19th, 1954, from the R.S.F.S.R. to the Ukraine, a change probably connected with Khrushchev's policy of upgrading his old Ukrainian fief, and comparable with the

---

[1] I have seen three copies of the 1941 edition of this production. In all of them, pp. 146 and 147, where the Volga German Republic was given, are stuck together with so great skill as to escape quite a careful look.

F

cession by Stalin of some of the other de-autonomized regions to his native Georgia. In neither case, of course, did the transfer bring any benefit to the deported peoples (nor, except in a prestige sense, to the republics gaining the territory).

There were, indeed, a few residual direct references to the deportees. The previous existence of their republics was not entirely suppressed in, for instance, the collection *The Communist Party of the Soviet Union in Resolutions and Decisions*. This quotes a decree of the Council of People's Commissars of the U.S.S.R. on grain cultivation. All the suppressed republics are mentioned in two tables (p. 839 and p. 846 respectively), the same as given in *Pravda*, June 30th, 1937. (The volume was passed for the press on September 25th to October 30th, 1953, and it also gives the fallen Beria's name in several contexts, quite apart from the decision of the Central Committee expelling him from the Party.) And there are passing references to the Chechen and Ingush languages in, for instance, *Languages of the North Caucasus and Daghestan*, published by the U.S.S.R. Academy of Science in 1949.

In the case of the Crimeans, the distant past was also too significant to be suppressed entirely, as we have seen already in the *Encyclopaedia*. At a 'Session on the History of the Crimea' reported in *Question of History*, No. 12 (1948), P. N. Nadinsky actually dealt with the difficulties caused by the 'persistence of survivals of capitalism in the minds of the Crimean Tatars'. And we also get such things as *Izvestia* of June 4th, 1952, carrying a historical article on the Crimea, whose theme was the Russian historical background of the area. Russians, the writer pointed out, had been settled there long before the arrival of the Tatars in the thirteenth century.

The one highly-publicized direct reference to any of the deported peoples was to a more or less historical theme, though its implications were plain. The Central Committee's decree of February 10th, 1948, on 'Decadent Trends in Soviet Music' to which we have already referred, attacked the opera *The Great Friendship*, by the Georgian composer V. Muradeli, *inter alia* because

The plot of the opera, which purports to portray the struggle for the establishment of the Soviet regime and the friendship of the peoples in the North Caucasus in the years 1918–20, is historically false and artificial. The opera creates the wrong impression that such Caucasian peoples as the Georgians and the Ossetians were at that time in enmity with the Russian people, which is historically false, inasmuch as it was the Ingushi and the Chechens who were during that period the obstacle to the establishment of the friendship of the peoples of the North Caucasus. (*Pravda*, February 11th, 1948.)

This statement, which contradicts all previous Soviet historical views, seems to have no purpose but to brand the Chechens and Ingushi as incurable recidivists on the one hand, and on the other to make it clear that nothing favourable about them, however true, would be permitted on the part of any Soviet writer. The branding of the whole of the past life of an individual who had strayed was old Stalinist practice, as in the cases of Trotsky and Bukharin. But the application of the principle to the past of whole nations was a new refinement in the rewriting of history.

A similar line was taken in the following years in professional circles. Among historians blamed for various ideological faults in 1949 was Professor I. M. Razgon, severely criticized for 'distorting' the history of the revolution in the North Caucasus. In a book published in 1941, *Ordzhonikidze and Kirov in the Struggle for the Soviet Regime in the North Caucasus*, he had depicted the Ingushi and Chechens as 'revolutionary'. At that time he presumably did not foresee that these nations would turn out to be the wrong people to praise. This manipulation of history was soon extended to an earlier period still, when, as we shall see later, the wars of the mountaineers against the Tsars came to be denounced.

A straightforward statement on the deportations themselves appears in a law book published in 1948. It may not be the only one, but such are certainly most rare. It is revealing:

In the background of the patriotic enthusiasm which inflamed the nations of the Soviet country united against the common enemy . . . there stand out strangely the monstrous, criminal and

treacherous acts of some small backward nations which gave
support to the enemy in the expectation of receiving 'privileges'
from him at the expense of the other nations of the Soviet Union.
These acts called for necessary and extraordinary measures by
the Soviet State in the interests of the U.S.S.R. as a whole and of
all the Soviet nations who remained faithful to their Fatherland
and to freedom; these measures consisted in the liquidation of
certain autonomous republics of the R.S.F.S.R. (for instance,
the Autonomous Republic of the Volga Germans, the Crimean
Autonomous Republic, and the Chechen-Ingush Autonomous
Republic). (A. A. Askerov and others, *Soviet State Law*, Moscow,
1948.)

The 'for instance' seems carefully phrased: only the liquida-
tions made public are named, but there is latitude for the
possibility of others having taken place. Here, too, the assertion
is made flatly that 'nations' and not just elements among them
gave support to the Germans. The privileges sought are not
stated. Nor is the fact that the nations were the majority of
those small enough to deport which had been reached by the
Germans.

Another law book lays down the motives and methods of
carrying out 'resettlement' for security purposes. Whether
based on the deportations or not, it certainly defines *ex post
facto* the Soviet legal, or at least actual, position:

Resettlement is carried out by the state organs of the U.S.S.R.:
(1) for the purpose of realizing measures connected with state
    security and defence of state frontiers and
(2) for the purpose of acquiring lands for agricultural pro-
    duction.
The first function is carried out by the organs of state security.
(Evtikhiev & Vlasov, *Administrative Law of the U.S.S.R.*, Moscow,
1946, p. 324.)

Such are the official statements, few and incomplete, in
which information about the nations and the Soviet attitude to
them could be read or deduced. In retrospect, indeed, certain
earlier statements gradually began to reveal their significance.
For instance, Ivan Serov was awarded the Order of Suvorov,
First Class, reserved for major victories in the field, on March
9th, 1944 — that is, immediately after the largest of his deporta-

tion operations, that of the Chechen-Ingush. (He was later made a Hero of the Soviet Union and received a number of other orders.)

On the whole, therefore, we see that almost nothing was publicly stated about the seven nations after they had gone into penal exile, except by implication. No news of their lives, or even their location, was allowed to be printed for ten years.

It is not easy to understand the motives for the publication of the Chechen-Ingush and Crimean decree, on the one hand, and the silence about the other nations on the other. We may perhaps take it that the single official announcement (which presumably became widely known in other minority territories — including areas like Lithuania where a partisan struggle was still being waged) was intended as a sharp reminder to the smaller Soviet nations. The silence apart from this single brief statement prevented any campaign against the deportations in the free world having a series of incidents to feed on. It was not, of course, that the Kalmyk, Karachai and Balkar deportations could be kept secret indefinitely, nor that fuller accounts of the Chechen-Ingush and Crimean affairs would not inevitably become available from scattered defectors. Yet single voices, able to tell usually only of events some years old, did not provide the stream of news' items which significant foreign interest needs to build up. Perhaps the brutal warning of the published decree had its intended effect internally. Certainly the studied silence which followed it, combined with the impermeability of the Soviet Union to investigation by free journalists, paid the Soviet leaders — up to a point.

Chapter 6

THE TRIAL OF SHAMIL

The only aspect of the whole business about which a good deal was written in the Soviet Union was in a historical polemic, starting in 1950, about what had hitherto been regarded as the proudest period in the history of the North Caucasus — the resistance to Tsarism led by Shamil. This retrospective purge of the Imam and his followers is of great significance in what it showed, and often asserted overtly, about Soviet nationality policy, and incidentally throws so much light on Soviet controversial methods, that it is worth looking at at some length.

In reality Shamil's main strength lay in Chechnia. But his movement covered a wide and multinational area of the North Caucasus, and he himself was an Avar from Daghestan. It was thus possible to attack him and his 'cult' without actual reference to the Chechens. And they are seldom if ever mentioned in the polemics, which either refer to 'the mountaineers' in general, or stick in a marked manner to references to Daghestani, or even Azerbaijani support for (or more usually oppression by) the Imam. He is treated, in fact, largely as the worst and most typical case of anti-Russian nationalism, and the habit of respecting him as a bourgeois-nationalist deviation of the worst sort. At the same time, it should be noted, lesser campaigns were being directed against smaller nuisances of nationalist history, like the Kazakh leader Kenesari Kasymov. In any case one would hardly be far wrong in regarding the Shamil tradition as exactly what had inspired the Chechens to resistance to Soviet rule, or in feeling that the Soviet rulers understood this point.

Even his contemporary opponents granted many admirable qualities to the Caucasian leader. Tolstoy, whose Caucasian tales must be one of the most remarkable feats of insight into the feelings and thought of a foreign people ever to have been performed, has a description of Shamil in Chapter 19 of his *Hadji Murad*. This is in 1852, after an unsuccessful campaign, when the Imam is shown exhausted by his difficulties, yet dignified and commanding. It is a restrained and quite unsentimental account, but the effect is a strong one, and probably as close to a reconstruction of the Caucasian hero as we are likely to see.

Tolstoy's account is more objective than that of Russians of the time less able to look at things *sub specie aeternitatis*. But still, his story was printed freely under the Tsars. The Tsarist regime had, too, spared the life of its most intransigent opponent when he was finally captured. And other Russian accounts give Shamil at least a certain admiration, however reluctant. It was not until 1950 that the successors of the Tsars retro-spectively proved (with 'documents') just how unforgivably criminal the Imam's resistance had been.

At first Soviet publications had been wholly enthusiastic about Shamil. In its article on *Shamil* the first edition of the *Large Soviet Encyclopaedia*, (Volume 61, 1934), says:

> The movement was aroused by the colonial policy of Russia, which robbed the basic population of their forests, tore away the best parts of their land for Cossack colonization, and in every way supported and sustained the despotism of the local feudalists. The popular rising carried out against Russia and against the local ruling strata was basically anti-feudal.

The article goes on to say that the social aims of the insur-gents were disguised in religious forms, and that the rising was carried on as a struggle against the Russians on the one hand and for the Shariya — Moslem law — on the other. It quotes Engels on the religious forms taken by the peasant risings in the Middle Ages, of which he had said 'from the equality of the sons of God they deduced civil equality'. The article adds, 'the idea of equality lay at the foundation of the interpretation of

Mohammedan theology by the popular masses of the Caucasus insurgent movement'. The Murid Kurali-Magoma is quoted as saying 'equality must exist among all Mohammedans'.

On Shamil himself it says that he showed the qualities of 'an outstanding political leader and a fine war chief', that he had 'enormous authority' among the masses and showed extraordinary personal heroism and skill, becoming a popular legend. His general ideas, and the religious-political organization he established to put them into practice, produced an extraordinary unity even in the 'multi-racial and multi-lingual Caucasus', which was united 'in one in the direct struggle against the colonial policy of Tsarism for its national liberation'. The article quotes Marx's dictum that Shamil was 'A great democrat'.

Even during the war against the Germans some use was made of the Shamil tradition. There was talk at the outset of the Caucasian mullahs proclaiming a Gazava — holy war — against the invaders. And Shamil's own name came in too. For instance the Daghestanis were reported as contributing 25,000,000 roubles to equip a tank column called 'Shamil' (E. Genkina, *Formation of the U.S.S.R.*, Moscow, 1943, p. 76).

Even after the deportations it was for a time possible for Soviet historians to describe events of past history from the anti-colonialist point of view. In A. M. Pankratova's *History of the U.S.S.R.* (Volume II, Moscow, 1947) there is still the old line on Shamil.

> Shamil was an outstanding political leader and military commander . . . Shamil was a gifted organizer of the state structure of the mountaineers and of their armed struggle against the Tsarist colonizers . . . The power of the beys and khans was liquidated everywhere . . . Shamil emancipated a considerable number of slaves . . . Shamil's action was directed at that time not only against Tsarism but also against the local feudal lords and was democratic and progressive.

On the war itself she mentions that in 1859 most of the villages of the Western Caucasus 'were burned and pillaged' and that between 1858 and 1864 400,000 mountaineers were deported from the Caucasus and their lands resettled with Russians.

Sporadic though unsupported attacks on Shamil were made as early as 1947 (e.g. *Questions of History*, No. 11, 1947), but in 1950 there came a total and officially dictated reversal of the previous view. Shamil was depicted for the first time as a pure reactionary, and an agent of foreign imperialism. It was first announced that the Stalin Prize awarded only the previous year to *From the History of Social and Philosophical Thought in Azerbaijan in the Nineteenth Century*, by Geidar Guseinov (Baku, 1949), had been withdrawn on account of his attitude to Shamil.

Pravda and *Izvestia*, on May 14th, 1950, reported that the Stalin Prize Committee 'in connection with the proposals of public organizations in Azerbaijan' discussed the question of Geidar Guseinov's book. It was now stated to be written 'from an incorrect political and theoretical standpoint' and particularly distorted the character of the Muridists, depicting them as progressive, democratic and national-liberationist. The author had said that Shamil 'in every possible way tried to help the Azerbaijanian peasants in their struggle against Tsarism' and had agreed with a bourgeois historian that Shamil 'is a hero and maker of heroes' and 'chosen of the people'. This evaluation was anti-Marxist and contradicted historical fact, because the movement was really reactionary and nationalist and 'in the service of British capitalism and the Turkish Sultan'. The Commission added, 'the idealization of Muridism in G. Guseinov's book is in essence a reflection of bourgeois-nationalist deviation and should be strongly condemned'. The nomination for the prize was withdrawn.

This sudden highly official pronouncement was followed by a great campaign to clean up Soviet historiography from the errors into which it had fallen on the subject. Daniyalov, the Party secretary in Daghestan (and now a full member of the Central Committee), repudiated Shamil. But the major statement in the Party's theoretical organ, *Bolshevik*, No. 13 (July 1950), was made by Bagirov, Party Secretary in Azerbaijan, and later to be shot as Beria's agent.

This 15,000-word article, *The Problem of the Character of the Movement of Muridism and Shamil*, which was cited continually in other periodicals in the campaign that followed, is a set piece of Stalinist methods, and deserves quoting at length:

> Lenin and Stalin teach that not every national movement is a progressive liberation movement. There are cases when national movements have a reactionary character, clash with the interests of development of the revolutionary movement and put a brake on the development of the class self-realization of the working people.
>
> History knows of many instances when foreign conquerors, colonizers and imperialists have organized and supported various movements, giving them a national or religious character, with the aims of usurpation in their struggle against their rivals.
>
> It is necessary to consider in this light and to criticize the mistaken conception, which has wide circulation in our Soviet historical literature, of the allegedly progressive, liberating character of the movement of Muridism and Shamil in the first half of the nineteenth century . . . .
>
> In the works of many Soviet historians (S. Bushuyev, R. Magomedov, M. Krovyakov and others), in the articles in the *Large Soviet Encyclopaedia*, in history textbooks for schools and higher educational institutions, Muridism and the Shamil movement are considered a liberating and progressive phenomenon. This anti-Marxist assessment of the movement of Muridism and Shamil found its reflection in the discussion 'On the Historical Essence of Caucasian Muridism', held in 1947 by the History Institute of the U.S.S.R. Academy of Sciences . . . .
>
> In order correctly to assess the movement of Muridism and Shamil, it is necessary to know that Muridism is a religious trend, one of the reactionary and warlike manifestations of Islam. As is well known, Islam arose in the seventh century in the feudal-merchant aristocracy which used Islam to unite the Arab tribes and to establish his power . . . .
>
> Muridism, the most warlike tendency in Islam, carried to extreme limits the religious intolerance expressed in the idea of a 'holy war' against the 'infidels'. From extant facts and documents it is evident that in implanting Muridism in the Caucasus the Turks and the British based their chief calculations on this aspect of Muridism — its intolerance of 'infidels' . . . .
>
> Shamil from the very beginning, like his predecessors, was closely linked with Turkey and acted in her interests . . . .
>
> For a loyal attitude to Russia, for the slightest suspicion of ties with the Russians, Shamil destroyed even the people of his own faith — Moslems. Shamil and his predecessors, Kazi Muhammed

and Gamzat Bek, dealt mercilessly with the population of villages and those individuals who refused to take part in the struggle against Russia . . . .

These examples provide one more proof that the Shamil movement was not one of liberation. Shamil did not consider it his task to liberate the mountain peoples. It was no accident that he did not obtain the support of the broad masses of the people of the Caucasus . . . .

Muridism was the domination of a small group of Murids, headed by the Imam, over the mass of Dagestani peasants . . . .

It is not true that Shamil destroyed all the feudal mountain lords. He persecuted and destroyed only those feudal lords who did not share his views and who opposed his activities . . . .

Apart from all the rest, Muridism and the Shamil movement sowed mistrust among the mountain tribes, hindered by that very fact their consolidation and unification and held up for many decades the economic and cultural development of the mountain peoples, which even without that were backward and ignorant. Is it really for these 'services' that certain comrades consider Shamil a national hero? How can one ignore all this numerous evidence and the facts and maintain that Shamil's 'rule' was democratic, and even go so far as to say that it was a people's republic, where the people themselves constituted the highest body of legislative power?

In such a situation it is completely beyond understanding that British lords and capitalists, who had oppressed subject peoples in their colonies by hundreds of thousands and millions, who had deprived them of their elementary human rights and privileges and sucked from them their very marrow, were supposed to help the 'national hero' Shamil, to nourish 'a special love' for the mountain nationalities and their 'liberation' movement.

In idealizing Shamil's personality not only bourgeois historians but even several of our Soviet historians go so far as to call Shamil a hero of heroes, a people's hero . . . .

What, however, is the reason that up to now the so-called Caucasian Muridism, the movement of the mountain tribes under the leadership of Shamil, has been so extolled, idealized and deceptively elucidated? It is the unscientific and uncritical attitude to this particular question; bourgeois objectivism in some and the manifestation of bourgeois nationalism in others in the elucidation of these events.

Many of our historians are in fact tied to the apron strings of bourgeois scientists, above all the British, and are held captive by a preconceived notion of Shamil as a national hero.

It is necessary to proceed to an assessment of Muridism and the movement among the mountain tribes headed by Shamil from the point of view of the general situation which was then taking shape in the South of Russia and in particular in the Caucasus.

In the eighteenth and the beginning of the nineteenth centuries the problem of their future fate faced the peoples of the Caucasus with particular acuteness. They could be swallowed up and enslaved by backward, feudal Turkey and Persia — or be annexed to Russia. Annexation to Russia was for the people of the Caucasus the only possible path for the development of their economy and culture. Inclusion in Russia created conditions for the liquidation of the economic and political parcelling out of the peoples of the Caucasus. The peoples of the Caucasus obtained security from external enemies.

Despite the arbitrary acts and cruelty of the Tsarist colonizers, the annexation of the Caucasus to Russia played a positive and progressive role for the peoples of the Caucasus . . . . The closeness to the Russian people, the joint struggle with the workers and peasants of Russia against the Tsarist autocracy and intercourse with advanced Russian culture and representatives of progressive, revolutionary social thought contributed to raising the material and spiritual culture of the peoples of the Caucasus and was a spur to the development of the revolutionary movement of the peoples of the Caucasus . . . .

The striving of advanced people in the Caucasus for union with Russia reflected the mood of the broad masses of the people.

After the annexation of North Azerbaijan to Russia the Azerbaijanis in the ranks of the Russian Army fought heroically against their centuries-old enemies, the Turkish and Persian usurpers . . . . After this, is not the statement by G. Guseinov the basest slander on the Azerbaijani people, viz. 'in its struggle against the Tsarist colonial regime and the local feudal lords, the Azerbaijan peasantry was inspired also by the movement of Shamil?'

In the light of all that has been said, how can we understand the positions of the officials of the History Institute of the U.S.S.R. Academy of Sciences, of the authors and editors of textbooks on the history of the U.S.S.R., Comrades Druzhinin, Pankratova, Zakhoder, Nechkina, Zaks and others, who idealize Muridism and distort historical truth, who extol the Muridism inspired by Russia's rivals, Turkey and Britain, and its leader Shamil?

The position of certain scientific workers and literary workers of Azerbaijan is also a manifestation of bourgeois nationalism: Mirza Ibrahimov, Mahmed Arif Dadash Zade and Mehti

Gusein, who have published favourable reviews and appraisals of Guseinov's wrong and harmful book.

Particular responsibility for the appearance in print and the popularization of Guseinov's book is borne by the editor of this book, A. O. Makovelsky, director of the Philosophy Institute of the Azerbaijan Academy of Sciences, Corresponding Member of the U.S.S.R. Academy of Sciences and member of the Azerbaijan Academy of Sciences, who, abusing his scientific and official position, has led our public into error . . . .

It is also impossible to overlook the position occupied by the U.S.S.R. Union of Soviet Writers regarding Guseinov's book. The Union of Soviet Writers put forward this book for the Stalin Prize competition without having examined its content and scientific value. Incidentally, this book does not have any direct connection with the work of the Union of Writers.

This extremely revealing document may thus be summarized:

(a) Some national movements are reactionary

(b) Muridism was one of these because it was anti-Russian, pro-British and Islamic

(c) Shamil and the Murids had no popular support, were undemocratic, and caused national dissension among the mountaineers

(d) The Tsarist annexation of the Caucasus was progressive, and supported by all advanced elements there

(e) Soviet historians had taken the opposite view, because of bourgeois nationalism, bourgeois objectivism and servility to the British

(f) They had better recant or else.

The article (which also attacked, for instance, a novel — *Shamil* by P. Pavlenko, published in 1941) struck the key-note for a major drive. It will only be worth referring to a few examples. The *Journal of the U.S.S.R. Academy of Sciences, Division of Literature and Language*, No. 3 (December 1950), publishes a decree of the Presidium of U.S.S.R. Academy of Sciences attacking a whole series of authors for 'politically pernicious' books about Shamil, ordering institutes concerned to hold meetings to discuss the question and to expose 'the reactionary nationalist substance of the Muridist Movement and Shamil'; ordering the editors of *Questions of History* to publish a series of articles attacking him; and dismissing R. M. Magomedov from the Vice-Chairmanship of the Dagestan branch of the Academy of Sciences for his 'bourgeois-nationalist interpretation' of the matter.

Fulfilling its instructions *Questions of History*, No. 10 (October 1950), publishes a long article on 'Sheikh Mansur and his Turkish inspirers'. Mansur was the early Murid leader of whom Tolstoy writes that the mountaineers held him to be a saint who had even stopped the local blood-feud system. The magazine conceded that he obtained the support of the 'backward mountain people' on account of the 'colonial policy of Tsarism, the endless confiscations and tribute'. The article says that Urshuma (i.e. Mansur) 'did not justify the hopes of the common people'. 'Instead of the struggle for land, against exploitation and for the idea of equality, Urshuma called for armed uprising against Russia . . . His uprising was a typical reactionary revolt directed by a foreign hand'. Many other magazines took up the affair. For instance *History Teaching in the School*, No. 6 (November-December 1950), attacks 'errors' on Shamil taught in the ninth grade of the secondary schools.

To support the charge that British incitement was the major factor in Shamil's movement, Soviet writers at this time made much of the travels and travel books of various Britons who had penetrated the region in the 1830's — E. Spencer, J. S. Bell, J. A. Longworth and in particular D. Urquhart, a keen champion of the North Caucasian cause who was even held partly responsible for Marx' and Engels' deviations on the subject.

The death of Stalin brought no immediate change of line on the Shamil issue. Historical works such as N. A. Smirnov's *Studies in the History of the Study of Islam in the U.S.S.R.* (Moscow, 1954) and S. K. Bushuev's *From the History of Foreign Political Relations at the Time of the Unification of the Caucasus and Russia* (Moscow, 1954) took the old anti-Muridist view very strongly, as did an article on the subject by A. V. Fadeev in *Questions of History*, No. 6 (1955).

The article already referred to on Caucasian Wars in the

second edition of the *Encyclopaedia*, Volume 19 (June 1953), says, 'But the unwillingness of the mountaineers to serve as cannon fodder for the Turkish Pashas and their Anglo-French allies wrecked the calculations of the Murid leaders'. It goes on: 'The struggle of the toiling mountaineers against the despotic regime and military theocratic dictatorship of Shamil weakened the power of the Imam and foretold his total defeat'. The Muridist movement is described simply in terms of 'Mohammedan fanaticism' and Shamil himself is bluntly called 'an Anglo-Turkish agent'.

Thus for six years, three under Stalin and three under his successors, the old hero, to whom even after the deportation of his Chechens, the intellectual spokesmen of the remaining Caucasians had continued to show their attachment, was treated as pernicious and vile. In spirit he too suffered deportation. But unlike the Chechens, he could still be spoken of, if only in a hostile fashion. And in their attitude to him the Soviet authorities demonstrated plainly what was felt about the Caucasian present as well as the Caucasian past. In effect Shamil was being blamed — *and in a sense rightly so* — for the resistance of the Chechens and others to the Soviet regime. When the restoration of nations took place, Shamil too, as we shall see, received rehabilitation, though of a partial and grudging nature. Meanwhile he stood as the diabolical incarnation of 'bourgeois nationalism'.

Chapter 7

UNOFFICIAL ACCOUNTS

U nofficial evidence about these nations has come in scrappy form from so many sources that in a work of this nature it has not been thought worth recording them. Individually, moreover, they are often unsubstantiated — an odd Austrian ex-prisoner-of-war in a newspaper interview mentioning that Chechens were to be found near the prison camp he was in in Karaganda, and so on. Yet reports of this sort check against each other, and some useful information emerges. It is worth noting, incidentally, that very little evidence of this sort became available during the first five or six years of these peoples' exile, partly because the prisoners-of-war from the penal areas did not start to get released until about then. This evidence, in any case, relates mainly to where the peoples were sent, which otherwise remained a complete mystery.

There are, however, a few non-Soviet sources whose information is more substantial: in particular, the account given by the ex-M.V.D. officer, Burlitski, and certain evidence collected by the magazines *Kavkaz* and *Prometheus*.

From Soviet official sources a perfectly clear picture can be constructed about the general nature of what happened to these peoples. But important points are missing. Not only are the destinations of the exiles not referred to, but there is little way of telling how the operations were carried out, both as a matter of police technique and from the point of view of the actual human suffering involved. On Soviet matters there are always certain readers who are not prepared to accept evidence which appears derogatory to the regime unless it is put out by the regime itself. This was seen for example, in the reception of Khrushchev's Secret Speech of February 1956, which after all only confirmed and gave detail of facts which were fairly generally known from unofficial evidence.

In a sense it is not unreasonable to stick to Soviet evidence on the principle which Gibbon puts forward of giving firm credit only to faults admitted by friendly, and to virtues conceded by hostile writers. But it seems to me that in view of the success of modern methods of news' suppression it would be applying it too scholastically if it led to the exclusion of any consideration whatever of the unofficial. So here I propose to abandon the principle for the moment, with the caveat — to readers who are not prepared to follow me — that this chapter does not pretend to conform to the rigorous methods of earlier and later ones, and if they wish to dismiss it they may. Its points are, however, reinforced occasionally by reference to official sources.

We may begin with a very brief look at the post-revolutionary history of the Northern Caucasus, as given by non-Soviet sources. It will have been seen already that Soviet accounts are incompatible with the deportations ever becoming necessary at all.

Official Soviet history, as given in earlier chapters, very occasionally contains or implies some reasons for disaffection on the part of these nations in spite of its strong insistence on the enthusiasm of the population for the regime. But less official accounts of the same period leave matters less contradictory. They may perhaps be defective or biased in certain respects, but they can scarcely be more so than the official ones, and will at least serve as a corrective.

On October 27th, 1917, a Congress of the Union of Peoples of the North Caucasus was held at Vedeno in Chechnia, Shamil's old capital, and the first point in its programme was:

All lands and forests proclaimed Tsarist property during the conquest of the Caucasus are returned to the nations from which they have been taken away.

It also proclaimed the political union of the area.

G

In March 1918 the Bolsheviks formed a Terek Province People's Soviet in Piatagorsk. The mountain peoples transferred their government to Temir-Khan-Shura (now called Buinaksk) in Daghestan. On May 11th, 1918, the North Caucasian Government proclaimed independence. It signed a treaty with Turkey in June and was recognized *de facto* by the other Central Powers. Its main difficulty was lack of armaments. Southern Russia was then full of Russian Army units supporting various White or Red authorities. The North Caucasian Government obtained arms for one brigade from the German authorities in the Ukraine. And a few hundred officers and other ranks of North Caucasian race who had been serving in the Turkish Army now returned to their native land. They included Colonel-General Berkuk, a Circassian.

From the start the new government was attacked by various White and Red Russian units and from February 1919 a continuous struggle against Denikin's White Army had to be undertaken. Denikin succeeded in occupying part of Chechnia and Daghestan as early as May, but in September and October his units suffered a number of defeats. During this struggle the mountaineers were naturally thrown into alliance with the Red forces. When Denikin had been defeated, however, the 11th Red Army repeated his invasion, occupying most of the country with little opposition at first, owing to being welcomed as allies.

In 1929 to 1930 both the Chechen-Ingush and the Kabardine-Balkar populations were in revolt for most of the winter. At one time almost the whole of Balkaria was in rebel hands.

The North Caucasus suffered very severely in the great purges of the late thirties. A 'nationalist conspiracy' on the part of local leaders had been discovered in 1934. In 1937 a mass attack was made on the whole of the leading cadres of the Chechen-Ingush republic. On the night of July 31st about 14,000 were arrested, of whom a large number were executed. *Pravda* on September 8th, 1937, published an article 'Bourgeois Nationalist Centre of Intrigues in Checheno-Ingushetia' which described terrorist operations by enemies of the people through-

out the Republic. It added that 'hostile elements have penetrated most greatly in those districts under the direct leadership
of the Chairman of the Executive Committee of the Chechen-
Ingush Autonomous Soviet Socialist Republic, Gorchkhanov,
the Second Secretary of the Regional Party Committee,
Bakhaev, and the head of the Agitprop Section, Oknev'. The
organ of the Regional Party Committee, *Groznyi Rabochii*,
according to Avtorkhanov (*National Murder in the U.S.S.R.*, in
Russian, Munich, 1952) spoke of the 'high protectors of the
subversive bourgeois nationalists' naming the above mentioned
and others. In October Shkiryatov arrived in Grozny and had
practically the whole of the local Communist leadership
arrested, including not only those already named but most of
the People's Commissars and a number of writers. 137 leaders
were charged with plotting to create a North Caucasian Republic under Anglo-Turkish protection. Gorchkhanov, his deputy
Salamov, and others were sentenced to death and the remainder
deported to labour camps. Avtorkhanov who had himself been
director of the Organisational Bureau of the Regional Committee of the Chechen Communist Party, states (Alexander
Uralov, *The Reign of Stalin*, London, 1953), that there were
about 120,000 arrests in the North Caucasus out of a population
of 3,000,000 in 1937-8, the 'General Operation' of summer
1937 producing about 100,000 of these. (We may here remark
that in the article on the Chechen Autonomous Province in the
first edition of the *Encyclopaedia* among the sources named is
Avtorkhanov's *On the Basic Problems of the History of Chechnia*
(Grozny, 1930). Curiously enough this book seems to be
referred to, though without its author's name, in a recent
collection, *Musical Culture of the Autonomous Republics of the
R.S.F.S.R.*)

The Karachai and Balkars had suffered in the collectivization troubles, and about 3,000 are said to have been shot
as a result of the 1929-30 rising. In 1937 the local administration was practically annihilated, and N.K.V.D. officers had
to take over direct rule in the area for some time. A practice at
this time which caused special resentment was the arrest of

women, which had previously been avoided, even under the Tsars.

Over the same period a strong campaign against Islam had resulted in the ten thousand odd mullahs of the North Caucasus shrinking to a few hundred with a similar handful of mosques. But Mohammedanism, lacking a hierarchy, is difficult to destroy, and the mountain peoples retained their religious attachments, as in fact about the only quasi-nationalist demonstration now not totally forbidden. In this unofficial and official accounts are at one — a thing especially objected to by the authorities being the survival, under the disguise of 'conciliation commissions', of the illegal Shariya courts, to which the Chechens voluntarily submitted their disputes.

In 1939 and 1940 there were further risings in the Caucasus. That of the Chechens was the most effective, though, as in 1930, trouble smouldered longest in the more inaccessible Balkar lands. Led by a former Communist, Hassan Izrailov, the Chechens held a considerable part of the mountain territory for some weeks and set up a provisional government. Several divisions, with air support, were concentrated against the rebels. But even after the country was largely subdued, small insurrectionary bands continued to operate in the depths of the forests.

The Kalmyks suffered severely in the collectivization drive. A decree of October 1929 on the expulsion of 'kulaks and feudalists' affected about 20,000 people, and a similar number died in the ensuing famine. As a result a Kalmyk Communist, Arash Chapchayev, openly called in 1933 for the reversal of collectivization, and there was a movement to reorganize the republic on the basis of the Mongolian People's Republic — then Sovietized but not collectivized — on the grounds that semi-nomad Kalmykia was economically comparable with the land of its co-nationals. The only result was a purge in which an estimated 5,000 perished, mainly Communist party members and intellectuals. During the same period the many lamaseries of the country were practically wiped out, and the Buddhist leaders mostly killed or driven into exile.

Crimean history, too, is inadequately covered in official accounts. On May 5th, 1917, 'A National Assembly' proclaimed the autonomy of the Crimean Tatars at Simferopol. In October a Kurultai proclaimed a Crimean Democratic Republic. This was rapidly suppressed by the communists and Chelebiev, the president, was shot in February 1918.

The Hungarian Communist Bela Kun, named head of the Crimean Revolutionary Committee, was despatched to the Crimea and instituted a reign of terror, which was met by a determined partisan movement. Lenin opposed this policy and an amnesty was proclaimed. However, with the beginnings of collectivization of agriculture, the pressure on the outlying nationalities was again increased. Waves of purges struck at the national leaders. At the time of the execution of Veli Ibrahim, for 'bourgeois nationalism', some thousands of Crimean Tatars were executed or deported.

In the following years the Soviet authorities continued this policy, which was marked by the deportation of 30,000 to 40,000 Crimean Tatars during the enforcement of collectivization. A rising took place in December 1930. Successive Tatar Presidents of the Crimean Republic were purged: Mehmed Kubay for protesting during the famine of 1931–34 that 'Moscow destroys the Republic of Crimea, carries away all its natural riches without giving bread to the starving population of the peninsula'; Ilias Tarakhan, his successor, and the Chairman of the Crimean Council of People's Commissars, Ibrahim Samedin, both of whom fell to the Yezhov mass terror of 1936–8, and were followed by a particularly large number of victims, even for those years. A 'special operation' against the Crimeans was mounted in December 1937.

In the circumstances, Soviet qualms about the loyalty of the Chechens and others became intense. The Ossetian, Colonel Tokaev, who had some access to what was being said in high political and military circles, has stated (in *Sotsialisticheskiy Vestnik*, No. 3, March 1951) that the Soviet General Staff reported in 1940 that the population of Northern Caucasus would prove a handicap in case of war and recommended that 'special measures' be taken in good time. It was not, of course, until the German threat had receded that any such measures were in fact taken. The actual decision to deport the Chechens is described by Tokaev as having been taken initially at a joint meeting of the Politbureau and High Command on February 11th, 1943, almost a year before it was put into effect. At this meeting, Tokaev states that Molotov, Zhdanov, Voznesensky, Andreyev and Kosygin (then Premier of the R.S.F.S.R.) urged the immediate and public liquidation of the A.S.S.R.; Mikoyan, while agreeing in principle that the Chechens should be punished, felt that such measures as deportation would be bad for the Soviet reputation; and Stalin, Voroshilov, Kaganovich, Khrushchev, Kalinin and Beria took the view that the Chechens would have to be deported eventually, but that this should be postponed until the Germans had been driven back further.

It is, of course, perfectly true that the Germans raised units from among the Chechens, as they did from most of the minority nations of the U.S.S.R. — and, indeed, from the Russians themselves. Their experience seems to have been that the Chechens fought with the utmost *élan* against Soviet units but that it was impossible to make them submit to German theories of discipline. There is an interesting account from the German side in *Wenn Sie Verderben Wollen* by Jürgen Thorwald (Stuttgart, 1952).

The deportation of the Volga Germans had, of course, already taken place before the decision on the other nations. Apart from their Volga Republic they had seventeen 'national districts' in other parts of the U.S.S.R. — mainly the Ukraine. The fate of these scattered Germans is hard to determine. Those who remained were taken back to Germany. But the deportation of the Volga Germans was ordered, as we have seen, in August 1941 when the Nazi penetration had not reached most of the German areas. It was plainly more urgent for the Soviet authorities to deport such Germans as were close to the front, and more likely to exert a diversionist influence on the fighting than those far back on the Volga, once they had made the assumption that German disloyalty was inevitable.

For some time the only fairly complete first-hand account of the non-German deportation operations was given by an M.V.D. defector, Colonel Burlitski, who took part in all of them except that of the Balkars. His story has been published in the West in *Life* on July 5th, 1954 and elsewhere. Before Khrushchev's Secret Speech it was only from such accounts that the dates of several of the deportations were definitely known. Khrushchev confirms our earlier evidence, giving in addition the Balkar date.

Dates of Deportations

	As given in the West 1953–6	*Khrushchev's Speech, February 1956*
Karachai - -	October/November 1943	end of 1943
Kalmyks - -	December 1943	December 1943
Chechens and Ingushi	February 23rd, 1944	March 1944
Balkars - -	Unknown	April 1944
Crimean Tatars -	June 1944	not mentioned
Volga Germans -	August 1941	not mentioned

A large number of Kabardines are also said to have been deported in March 1944. Since this date was given long before Khrushchev made the date of the Balkar deportation available it seems that they went along with the smaller members of the Republic. As Mr Walter Kolarz says in his *Russia and Her Colonies* (p. 193) the Kabardines exhibited much 'disloyalty' during the war with Germany, and though this was not on a scale to get them deported *en bloc* as a nation considerable drafts seem to have been sent to Kazakhstan, apparently the Dzhambul area.

The M.V.D. concentrated for the deportation operations a large part of the military forces under their command — Border Troops, Interior Troops, Convoy Troops, and the 'Special Purpose' Troops whose main task during the war had been to remain in the rear of fighting units with the purpose of rounding up and executing them if they retreated without orders. The most notorious of these formations, the First Special Purpose Division (D.O.N.) seems to have carried out the more unpleasant tasks of deportation. The method employed was for the units to be brought into the area some weeks before the operation with the purpose of making detailed plans and familiarizing themselves with the position. When action commenced each village was surrounded by armed troops, and a number of soldiers detached to accompany the 'operational' security-police officers each detailed to round up the families in a given group of houses. In the case of the Karachai and Kalmyks the decree was formally read in the villages and each family was allowed a hundred kilograms of property, including food. The inhabitants were then assembled in fields or other convenient places where they remained, often for a day and night, before the transport columns appeared to take them to the railhead. In these cases the population allotted to each regiment appears to have been in the nature of two to five thousand, which gives some idea of the size of the forces involved.

The (unpublished) decree deporting the Kalmyks is reported as having been dated December 27th, 1943. The order removing Kalmyks from the army does not seem to have been put out until the following month. The Kalmyks, perhaps in accordance with their Buddhist principles, are said to have accepted their fate quietly. A number of leading Kalmyks had been able to retreat with the German armies. The Calcutta *Statesman* of May 4th, 1955, states that about 1,300 of them belong to the main émigré organization. And they have conducted considerable and effective publicity in the countries of Asia, under their leader, Dr. Naminow and others.

The remaining deportations caused a considerable amount of sporadic fighting, but on the whole surprise was effected. It is extraordinary to consider the circumstances that must have prevailed for the Chechens not to have been forewarned by news of the earlier deportations, and to have been caught off guard. But all accounts agree that the N.K.V.D. units, dressed as ordinary troops, entered the republic in early February 1944, as if for manoeuvres. The population was assembled in the villages on February 23rd, 1944, to celebrate Red Army Day. They were surrounded by troops and the deportation decree was read to them by security officers. Stormy scenes ensued, in which many of the weaponless Chechens and Ingushi were shot down. The rest were rounded up and allowed to collect 50 kilograms of baggage per family (or according to some accounts 40 kilograms — in any case less than the Kalmyks). They were then driven away in trucks — mainly lease-lend Studebakers, we are told by Lt.-Col. Burlitski, who took part in the deportation of the Chechen village of Novoselskoye. This was organized by General Serov from his headquarters at Grozny, in which town, at a special meeting, the Republic's Ministers, the Presidium of its Supreme Soviet, and the Provincial Committees of the Communist Party and the Young Communist League were put under arrest — good practice for the later trapping of Pal Maleter in Budapest.

Russian students at Grozny were sent to look after the farms in the valleys until labour could be brought in from Russia proper, and isolated mountain farms were burnt to stop use of them by 'bandits'. For a number of Chechens escaped, apart from those who for one reason or another had remained outside the villages.

The Karachai and Balkars had been the object of particularly lawless N.K.V.D. activity without a pause for several years. During the fighting in the territory in the war, there were a number of cases of whole villages being subjected to pogroms by retreating N.K.V.D. units. And on their return a good deal of punitive fighting and burning went on till order was restored, of which advantage was finally taken to deport the survivors. Even after that some resistance continued. And Karachai losses, in the actual process of deportation, are said to have been particularly heavy owing to the exceptional brutality resulting from this. As late as February 1951, it is said that numbers of Chechens and Balkars were still living an outlaw existence in the mountains.

During the winter journey of the deportees in cattle-trucks, which lasted several weeks, deaths are reported to have run as high as 50 per cent, mainly old people, but including numerous typhus victims of all ages.

The Crimean deportations followed the German evacuation of the area much more rapidly than in the other cases. The Crimea was only fully liberated in April 1944, and the Crimeans were removed in June, among them the members of the small pro-Soviet partisan movement, including its leader, Khaurullakh. This deportation seems to have been carried out with an accompaniment of much killing and brutality.

Reports of returned Austrian and German prisoners-of-war and of Soviet subjects who have escaped from the U.S.S.R., give some idea, belatedly enough, of where the deported nations disappeared to. Their account has been supplemented by a few Western journalists, such as Mr. Harrison Salisbury of the *New York Times*, who visited certain of the areas concerned.

In general the bulk of the Chechens and Ingushi were sent to Kazakhstan and Kirghizia. This is certainly an enormous area. But the scattering of the Volga Germans and the Crimean Tatars was over a wider region. It is reported that the Sverdlovsk area was main initial centre of Crimean Tatar deportation, but they have also been noted in Birobidzhan, in Yakutia, near Kostroma in European Russia, at Karaganda in Kazakhstan, at Taishet, near Irkutsk, near Lake Issyk-Kul in Kirghizia, and in Uzbekistan. That is, over almost the whole stretch of Siberia and Central Asia and in the northern part of European Russia as well. Of those deported to Uzbekistan it is said that about 20 per cent died during the first year.

Volga Germans are equally reported over a very wide area. There were, of course, more of them — especially if we include Germans deported from other areas who might well be mentioned under the same general term. It seems not unlikely that returning prisoners-of-war especially may have been more alert to the presence of their co-linguists. In any case, many more reports of their presence have been published — from Kostroma, Kemerovo, Yakutsk, Krasnoyarsk, Chelyabinsk, Novosibirsk, Karaganda, Balkash, Temir Tau, Kustanai and elsewhere. Here again practically all the possible territories seem to have received scattered groups. It is incidentally reported that the Volga Germans were not subject to military call-up until 1954 when they were once again taken into the forces for menial tasks.

The Caucasian mountaineers are mainly reported in Kirghizia and Kazakhstan. The few exceptions (near Sverdlovsk in European Russia and near Irkutsk in Siberia) were in special labour camps and seem to have been Chechens sent away under arrest immediately after the restoration of order in the republic and prior to the mass deportations. Those withdrawn from the Army at the time of the deportation seem to have been sent first to Kostroma in European Russia and from there, after an interval, into Central Asia. Chechens and Ingushi are reported, often intermixed with other populations, from the area west of Frunze in Kirghizia, and from the Akmolinsk, Karaganda, Aktyubinsk, Kustanai and Petropavlovsk areas in the Kazakh S.S.R. There have been several accounts of a rising of Ingushi at Borovoye in the north of Kustanai Province of Kazakhstan in the spring of 1945. It seems to have been put down with considerable bloodshed. At Krasnoyarsk about 4,000 Chechens were in penal camps. In October 1954 a successful rising in one of these camps led to a break-out and attacks on the others in which finally most of the prisoners became involved. A large proportion escaped. Mopping-up operations went on for several months, but a number of Chechens were never captured.

Very little has been heard of the Karachai and less of the Balkars. One of the few items published in this country about the Karachai, for instance, appears on page 222 of *Vanished without Trace* by Antoni Ekart (London, 1954), which recounts his experiences in a Soviet labour camp. One of his fellow prisoners was a girl, Khabicheva, a Karachai from Mikoyan Shakhar who had been arrested before the deportation of her race and had been for over a year trying to find out where they had been sent. She finally discovered that they were in Kazakhstan and Kirghizia. Karachai, and possibly also Balkars, have been reported by others in the area of Kazakhstan between Dzhambul and the Kirghiz border. (It seems possible that, as

The Deportations

Reported Areas
of Exile

- - - - Crimean Tatar
· · · · · Kalmyk
————— Volga German
— · — · — Chechen-Ingush
ʌʌʌʌʌ Karachai-Balkar

to Yakutia and
elsewhere

Krasnoyarsk
Kemerovo
Novosibirsk
Barnaul
Temir Tau

MONGOLIA

CHINA

ALTAI TERR.

Semipalatinsk

Petropavlovsk
Omsk

Karaganda
Akmolinsk

Balkhash

Lake Balkhash

Alma Ata

Lake Issyk-Kul

KIRGIZISTAN

Dzhambul

TADZHIKISTAN

Chelyabinsk

Kustanai
Kokchetav

Aktyubinsk

K A Z A K H S T A N

UZBEKISTAN

Aral
Sea

TURKMENISTAN

IRAN

Samara
Volga

Saratov

Stalingrad

CASPIAN SEA

Kostroma

Moscow

Don

UKRAINE

BLACK SEA

TURKEY

Turkic speakers they would be likely to be confused in other reports with 'Tatars' in general.) A Balkar location is confirmed by a member of Sir John Hunt's British Caucasian Expedition in 1958. At first an attempt was made to explain dilapidation in the Balkar area to him as the result of landslides, but finally Balkar shepherds told him of the deportations. They had been 'invited to a rally. Everyone came. When we got there troops surrounded us and the whole tribe was told that as we had co-operated with the Germans, we were to be punished and deported to Central Asia'. There they lived 'beside the shores of Issyk-Kul'. ('Climbing with the Russians' by Ralph Jones, the *Geographical Magazine*, June 1959.) According to these Balkars conditions in their area of exile had, in recent years at least, been good.

There has been remarkably little information on the Kalmyks. It seems in the first place that their deportation was carried out with exceptional brutality or inefficiency and that the death rate was higher in their inhospitable Siberian reception area even than that associated with the other deportees. A fair number of them seem to have ended up in the Krasnoyarsk area in Siberia.

Estimates of the total number of deaths during the journey and in the first and most difficult year of resettlement vary to some extent with the area, but most of the figures are close to two-fifths of the populations concerned, old people and children suffering most. If we could accept this as a rough average it would imply casualties amounting to about half a million.

It will be seen that certain areas such as Karaganda received an influx of all sorts of races. Karaganda is the centre of one of the main labour camp complexes of the Soviet Union. And with its 'free' deportee population too, it seems to have become a human dumping ground. It appears to be usual for deportees, here and elsewhere, to have to report to the police at intervals. In common with the whole of the rural population of the U.S.S.R. they have been unable, under the passport regulations, to move from their settlements without permission.

Conditions reported vary between 'fair' for Chechens in the

Frunze province of Kirghizia to 'very bad', little food, mud huts and so on for those in the Akmolinsk province of Kazakhstan. Disease 'due to under-nourishment' was said to be rampant in the Aktyubinsk province of Kazakhstan in 1955 among Chechens. All reports agree that these peoples remained extremely anti-Soviet.

The work on which deportees were engaged was mainly in agriculture. Some, however, were directed to mines. And they also formed a pool for labour on canals and railway construction. The railway from Frunze to Ribachye on Lake Issyk-Kul, for instance, a difficult task involving cuttings through the gorges, was carried out almost entirely by Chechen, Ingush and Tatar labour.

The Volga German Republic was occupied by N.K.V.D. troops in August 1941. Property was confiscated, and the inhabitants, in some areas at least, then given two hours' notice to move. In theory an allowance of a ton of luggage per family was permitted, much greater than was later to be the rule with the Asian peoples. There were a number of shootings, mainly as the result of the work of agents-provocateurs pretending to be German agents. But with the move itself the formalities were observed of stating that a simple transfer was envisaged, and that all property confiscated would be replaced in the reception areas.

The trains took a very long time. One German deportee from Mariupol speaks of a fortnight between that city and Penza, merely. On arrival in Kazakhstan and elsewhere reports are unanimous that the Germans were well treated by the local population, in spite of its own poverty. But it was a frightful ordeal, even so.

Wolfgang Leonnard, in his *Child of the Revolution* (London, 1957) describes a brief visit in 1941 to one of the deportation areas for Germans. He himself was a Communist and, though most even of the German Communists in Moscow were being compulsorily resettled, he was himself technically exempt, being required as a propagandist by the Russians. But he was induced to travel with the deportees and describes how after twenty-two days in a cattle-truck with some fifty others they arrived near Ossokarovka, about seventy-five miles north of Karaganda. Before he managed to extricate himself he was marched with the others about fifteen miles to 'Settlement no. 5'. This was an area to which, in the early thirties, deported kulaks had been sent. When these had arrived, they told Leonnard, there was nothing but bare ground. They had dug holes in the earth to live in. Many had died of cold and hunger, but by now they had constructed clay huts and the survivors were scraping a living. The Germans had been billeted on these outcasts. The huts were of mud, without windows and with a single opening which was simply stopped up in winter. When Leonnard had managed to get to Karaganda he met various other Germans who had been in these places. Many of them were getting far less than their minimal official ration and had been allotted huts and outhouses which even the kulak deportees no longer found habitable. The cold was, at this time, becoming intense.

This early deportation of the Germans was more a precaution than a punishment. And their treatment was throughout better than that of later deportees. In many cases these were not billeted anywhere. They were simply marched to empty stretches of country, given agricultural implements and told to produce. In fact, they were subjected to the same measures as the original kulak deportees, and the survivors built themselves the same holes in the ground and mud huts.

This applied even to the Greeks, who were deported long after the war, when it might have been thought possible to make better arrangements. But, if it comes to that, there have recently been complaints from the new 'volunteer' settlers on the Virgin Lands, who are supposed to be under special Government auspices as an *élite* of Young Communists, that everything is lacking in their new settlements. If even favoured groups are so neglected, it is not to be expected that much trouble should be taken about the deportee pariahs.

The deportation of the Greeks, which took place in 1949, has never been mentioned officially in the U.S.S.R. The article on Greeks in the second edition of the *Large Soviet Encyclopaedia*

(Volume 12, passed for press on May 28th, 1952) mentions the
existence of Greeks in the Soviet Union in the form that there
are Greeks outside Greece and Cyprus 'in Turkey (in Istanbul),
in Egypt (particularly Alexandria), in the U.S.S.R. and elsewhere'. It may be of some significance that, unlike the case
with Turkey and Egypt, no reference is made to the *location* of
the Soviet Greeks. In fact before deportation they lived almost
entirely on the coasts of the Black Sea and the Sea of Azov —
Mariupol, now called Zhdanov, being at one time an almost
wholly Greek city. The equivalent article in the first edition
of the *Encyclopaedia*, Volume 19, mentions them in Mariupol
(64,238 of them), other regions of the Ukraine (72,032) and
the Caucasus (52,654) with others scattered elsewhere.

There is one small piece of published information which
may refer to the deportation of the Greeks. *Izvestia* of October
4th, 1949, lists a series of awards made to officers of the M.V.D.
and M.G.B. for carrying out 'a special Government mission':
two Lieutenant-Generals and three Major-Generals are named.
Few security operations had been carried out recently on a
scale involving such a number of high officers. The 'Leningrad
Affair', which is said to have resulted in the shooting of up to
3,000 members of the Communist Party in that city, was then
still under way, and on the face of it would anyhow seem to
have been an M.G.B. operation pure and simple. It is true
that operations against partisans, and mass deportations, were
then taking place in the Baltic States as well. But it is at least
possible that the Greek operation is referred to.

The award of high orders to the police generals in charge of
deportations is certainly traditional. Serov, who immediately
after the Chechen-Ingush operation received the Order of
Suvorov, officially reserved for major victories in the field, was
in charge of all the deportations and then of anti-partisan
activity in Lithuania. His chief subordinates, Goglidze and
Gvishiani, were also decorated, as was Kobulov, who is believed
to have assisted in the Crimean deportation. These three were
later shot. But Serov survives and has not, at the time of
writing, been required to turn in the decoration received for

what has now been admitted to be a crime for over two years.

The deportation of the Greeks — together with many Turks and Persians who inhabited the Caucasian region — was the last of the major operations. The Greek population of the U.S.S.R. was 285,000 in 1940. The Greeks in the Crimea, about 10,000 in number, had already been sent to Kazakhstan in 1944.

Many from other areas had been sent east earlier, and others had left the country. There remained about 40,000 Greeks in the Caucasus — mainly in the towns of the Black Sea Coast of Georgia. These were rounded up at two hours' notice on June 14th, 1949. They were sent mainly to Kazakhstan.

More has been heard from them than from most of the deportees, owing to their links with their homeland. (About 17,000 of them were actually Greek citizens.) They were able to smuggle a few letters to relations. Two of these may be quoted as descriptions which must stand for the fate of the many other races who had preceded them to Kazakhstan. One tells of the deportation itself:

> We travelled seventeen days, exposed to cold, hunger and thirst. Many of our fellow deportees died in the trains . . . . We have been brought into the desert. There are no built-up houses. The water is not drinkable and many children have already died.

The following from another letter gives some idea of the conditions of exile:

> At the Kolkhoz where we are forced to work the norms are very high. For a 'day's wage' we have to do the equivalent of three or four days' work. For one 'day's wage' they give us a kilo of corn and nothing more . . . . There is no firewood in this desert. What shall we do during the winter?

H

Chapter 8

COMMUNISM AND THE NATIONAL QUESTION

As the small peoples of the Caucasus and the Crimea thus went for years and decades into the oblivion of a miserable exile, some of those who learned of the deportations may have wondered how they could be reconciled with the 'Socialist humanism' often mentioned in the Soviet press, or even with Marxist principles.

And yet the Soviet regime has never undertaken measures, however ruthless, of which it cannot be argued that they are in accord with its theoretical principles. Its treatment of the Chechens and other nations has political and ideological roots which go deep into the whole Marxist-Leninist outlook. What is basic is that the Communists' attitude to national sentiment is centred on the fact that they regard it as subsidiary and temporary. In its article on 'Nation' the *Large Soviet Encyclopaedia* (2nd edition, Vol. 29 (November 1954), p. 307) says:

> Nations first arose in the period of the liquidation of feudalism and the development of capitalism. People consolidated themselves into nations not in accordance with their own desires, by the will of governments or the activity of any other subjective factors, but only as the result of the action of the objective laws of economic development.

This is merely restating Stalin's dictum: 'A nation is not merely a historical category, but a historical category belonging to a definite epoch, the epoch of rising capitalism'. (Stalin, *Marxism and the National and Colonial Question* (1913), p. 13.)

Lenin made the same point, though in an even more crudely 'economic' way when he said:

> Throughout the world, the period of the final victory of capitalism over feudalism was linked up with national movements. The economic basis of these movements is that in order to achieve complete victory for commodity production the bourgeoisie must capture the home market, must have politically united territories with a population speaking the same language, while all obstacles to the development of this language and to its consolidation in literature are removed. (Lenin, *Selected Works*, Vol. 4, p. 250.)

Thus the Communists regard the nation as a phenomenon arising at a certain stage of historical development. Nations, and their wish for independent sovereign States, did not exist before bourgeois class-consciousness; and in post-bourgeois times, when the Communists are in control, national consciousness will become obsolete. As Lenin says:

> The aim of Socialism is not only to abolish the present division of mankind into small States, and all-national isolation, not only to bring the nations closer to each other, but also to merge them. (Lenin, 1916, *Selected Works*, Vol. 5, p. 270.)

He elsewhere maintains that capitalism has two effects on the development of nations. It not merely produces them, but also accelerates the breakdown of national barriers so that it destroys national seclusion and substitutes class antagonism for national antagonism. 'It is therefore perfectly true that in the developed countries the working men have no country' (Lenin, *Selected Works*, Vol. 11, p. 352). The national question is thus seen as an inessential survival and as part of the epoch of 'bourgeois democratic' revolution rather than one which concerns the final state of the proletarian revolution. On the issue in Russian circumstances Lenin says:

> In eastern Europe and in Asia the period of bourgeois-democratic revolutions started only in 1905. The revolutions in Russia, Persia and China, the wars in the Balkans, such is the chain of world events of *our* period in our 'Orient'. And only the blind can fail to see the awakening of a *whole series* of bourgeois-

democratic national movements, striving to create nationally independent and nationally united States in this chain of events. It is precisely and solely because Russia and the neighbouring countries are passing through this epoch that we require an item in our programme on the right of nations to self-determination. (Lenin, 1914, *Sochineniya*, 20, p. 378.)

Support for national movements of the type now described by Lenin as arising in the peripheral nationalities of Russia, like the Chechens and Crimeans, is thus regarded by Communists as tactically necessary only in an intermediate stage. Where this stage can be avoided, as in dependent countries with no active bourgeoisie, the question need never arise. An example given by Lenin from Marx is:

If capitalism in England had been overthrown as quickly as Marx first expected, there would have been no place for a bourgeois-democratic and general national movement in Ireland. But since it arose, Marx advises the British workers to support it . . . . (Lenin, 1914, *Sochineniya*, 20, p. 411.)

Having admitted that national aspirations do exist over an undefined transitional period, Lenin immediately considers how to utilize them. It was, indeed, in connection with nationalist movements that he said:

The General Staffs in the present war assiduously strive to utilize all national and revolutionary movements in the camp of their enemy: the Germans utilize the Irish Rebellion, the French — the Czech movement, etc. From their standpoint they are acting quite properly. A serious war would not be treated seriously if advantage were not taken of the slightest weakness of the enemy, if every opportunity that presented itself were not seized, the more so since it is impossible to know beforehand at what moment, where and with what force a powder magazine will 'explode'. We would be very poor revolutionaries if, in the great proletarian war for emancipation and Socialism, we did not know how to utilize *every* popular movement against *each separate* disaster caused by imperialism in order to sharpen and extend the crisis. (Lenin, 1916, *Selected Works*, Vol. 5, p. 305.)

The crux of the matter is thus established — national movements and questions of national sovereignty are transitional phenomena of a bourgeois nature, but ones which can be utilized by the Communists in their conduct of the more important class struggle. From this the perfectly natural conclusion was drawn that it might or might not be possible to turn particular national movements to the advantage of the Communists. And those which could not be so used were to be ruthlessly opposed. Even before the Russian revolution Lenin said:

> If . . . a number of peoples were to start a Socialist revolution . . . and if *other* peoples were found to be serving as the main bulwarks of bourgeois reaction — then we would be in favour of a revolutionary war against the latter, in favour of 'crushing' them, destroying all their outposts, no matter what small national movements arose . . . .

on the grounds that

> The various demands of democracy, including self-determination, are not an absolute, they are a particle of the general democratic (at present general Socialist) world movement. In individual concrete cases, a particle may contradict the whole; if it does, then it must be rejected. (Lenin, 1916, *Sochineniya*, 22, p. 326.)

And any particular national movement might be sacrificed, on the principle that:

> . . . the interests of the democracy of *one* country must be subordinated to the interests of the democracy of *several and of all* countries. (Lenin, 1916, *Sochineniya*, 22, p. 330.)

Lenin was not, of course, doing anything very new. Marx and Engels had supported the Polish and Hungarian national movements of the previous century, but had opposed those of the Czechs and South Slavs, as Stalin points out:

> In the 'forties of the last century Marx supported the national movement of the Poles and Hungarians and was opposed to the national movement of the Czechs and the South Slavs. Why? Because the Czechs and the South Slavs were then 'reactionary nations'. (Stalin, *Works*, Vol. 6, p. 147.)

In Marx's time it was, of course, the Germans who were thought of as the progressive nation, and Marx said that

Except for the Poles, the Russians, and at best the Slavs in Turkey, no Slavic people has a future, for the simple reason that all Slavs lack the most basic historic, geographic, political and industrial prerequisites for independence and vitality. (Marx, 'Democratic Panslavism', *Neue Rheinische Zeitung*, February 1849.)

Engels even wrote,

Now you may ask me whether I have no sympathy whatever for the small Slavic peoples, and remnants of peoples . . . . In fact, I have damned little sympathy for them. (Engels, Letter to Kautsky, February 7th, 1882.)

Lenin, too, approved this early discrimination between nations on tactical or economic grounds. For example, he points out that Marx supported the liberation movement in Poland merely as a temporary expedient until progress should take place in Russia, after which Poland would lose its importance — for the good Marxist reason that Russia was a more industrialized Power. Basing himself on previous Marxist teaching he insisted that:

As long as the masses of the people in Russia and in most Slavic countries were still fast asleep, as long as *there were no* independent, mass, democratic movements in these countries, the *aristocratic* liberation movement in Poland assumed enormous, paramount importance . . . .
In general the attitude of Marx and Engels to the national question was strictly critical, and they recognized its historical relativity. Thus, Engels wrote to Marx on May 23rd, 1851, that . . . the significance of Poland was temporary, that it would last only until the agrarian revolution in Russia. . . . In Russia there were more elements of civilization, education, industry and of the bourgeoisie than in 'aristocratic Poland'. (Lenin, *Sochineniya*, 20, pp. 403, 406.)

The view of the sacrifice of national to other considerations put forward by Lenin was developed at length by Stalin, who became the Bolshevik theorist on the national question — and remains so to this day.

Some of Stalin's works, such as the *Short Course History of the Communist Party* and *Economic Problems of Socialism* have been repudiated by the present regime. But his formulations on the national question have not been criticized in any way and remain entirely authoritative. Indeed, it would be difficult for this to be otherwise, since the crucial essay in *Marxism and the National and Colonial Question* was written in pre-revolutionary times and approved by Lenin. And Lenin, of course, appointed him Commissar for Nationalities in the first Soviet Government in 1917.

Dotting the i's of Lenin's theories, Stalin writes,

> This does not mean, of course, that the proletariat must support *every* national movement, everywhere and always, in every individual concrete case. It means that support must be given to such national movements as tend to weaken, to overthrow imperialism, and not to strengthen and preserve it. Cases occur when the national movements in certain oppressed countries come into conflict with the interests of the development of the proletarian movement. In such cases support is, of course, entirely out of the question; The question of the rights of nations is not an isolated, self-sufficient question; it is a part of the general problem of the proletarian revolution, subordinate to the whole, and must be considered from the point of view of the whole. (Stalin, *Problems of Leninism*, 1924, p. 74.)

And again:

> It should be borne in mind that in addition to the right of nations to self-determination, there is also the right of the working class to consolidate its power, and the right of self-determination is subordinate to this latter right. There are cases when the right of self-determination conflicts with another, a higher right — the right of the working class that has come to power to consolidate that power. In such cases — this must be said bluntly — the right of self-determination cannot and must not serve as an obstacle to the working class in exercising its right to dictatorship. (Stalin, *Works*, Vol. 5, p. 270.)

This theme, so often repeated, is absolutely basic to the Communist view of the nation. How consistently it has been maintained may be seen by comparing the passages from Stalin and Lenin with an article which appeared after Stalin's death in *Kommunist*, No. 15 (October 1953): 'Socialist Nations of the U.S.S.R. under Conditions of Transition from Socialism to Communism', by M. Kammari, which repeated the views of

Stalin on nationality. The striking thing is that in this very long article Stalin himself is not mentioned at all while Lenin is quoted frequently. As Stalin had long been the official expert on nationalities, the omission of reference to him can scarcely have been unintentional. And it seems to imply that he was then not well regarded by his successors. In general references to Stalin reached a very low point in the summer of 1953. What is significant is that while thus, in effect, repudiating the dead dictator, his basic thesis on the subordination of national rights to the interests of the Party was still strongly insisted on: 'The national question is subordinated to the more general and fundamental question of the socialist revolution and the Dictatorship of the Proletariat'. In addition the article makes the other old points — about the progressive role of Russian influence in the history of the minorities even in Tsarist times, about the dangers of bourgeois nationalism ('tendencies . . . engendered by pressure from the exploiting classes and their agents who incite national difference and enmity among the working people of various nationalities with a view to restoring capitalism') and so on.

The general thesis that reactionary nations should not have their interests considered, which is still correct doctrine, had been put forward, as we have seen, even before there was a 'socialist' state, at a time when 'progressive' countries simply had larger proletariats or bigger socialist parties. *A fortiori*, when one state is actually in the power of the Communist Party the interests of rival nations are not to be considered where they clash with those of the Communist state — particularly as it is in the interests of the revolution for the latter to enlarge itself. Immediately after the revolution, Lenin wrote,

> There is not a single Marxist who, without making a total break with the foundations of Marxism and Socialism, could deny that the interests of Socialism are above the interests of the right of nations to self-determination. Our Socialist Republic has done and is continuing to do everything possible for implementing the right of self-determination for Finland, Ukraine, etc. But if the concrete position that has arisen is such that the existence of the Socialist Republic is endangered at a given moment in respect

of an infringement of the right to self-determination of a few nations (Poland, Lithuania, Courland, etc.) then it stands to reason that the interests of the preservation of the Socialist Republic must take preference. (Lenin, *Works*, Vol. 26, p. 408.)

Not only did all national movements opposed to Soviet centralism automatically become subject to legitimate destruction on the grounds that they hampered progress to 'Socialism', but it was definitely stated that national aspirations to sovereignty and independence in areas which the Tsars had ruled were reprehensible and meaningless. Stalin issued the simple ultimatum:

> When a life-and-death struggle is developing between proletarian Russia and the Imperialist *Entente*, there are only two possible outcomes for the border regions:
> *Either* they go along with Russia, and then the toiling masses of the border regions will be freed from imperialist oppression;
> *Or* they go along with the *Entente*, and then the yoke of imperialism will be inevitable.
> There is no third course. The supposed independence of supposedly independent Georgia, Armenia, Poland, Finland, etc., is only an illusion, and conceals the utter dependence of these apologies for States on one or another group of imperialists. (Stalin, 1920, *Works*, Vol. 4, p. 365.)

Indeed even the formation of States such as Czechoslovakia and Yugoslavia, outside the old Russian sphere,

> did not, and could not, bring about the peaceful co-existence of nationalities; it did not, and could not, eliminate either national inequality or national oppression, for the new national States, being based on private property and class inequality, cannot exist: (*a*) without oppressing their national minorities . . . (*b*) without enlarging their territories at the expense of their neighbours, which gives rise to conflicts and wars . . . and (*c*) without submitting to the financial, economic and military domination, of the 'great' imperialist Powers. (Stalin, 1921, *Works*, Vol. 5, pp. 18–19.)

This schematic attitude to national sentiment, on the part of politicians who themselves had little use for it, resulted in an underestimate of its powers. This misevaluation has bedevilled

Communist policy for decades; yet it is repeated again and again, as in Hungary. An explicit analysis of what measures would be enough to satisfy national feeling was made by Stalin early in his career, and became the basis of Soviet tactics in attempting to appease the minorities. Its inadequacy is startling:

> A minority is discontented not because there is no national union but because it does not enjoy the right to use its native language. Permit it to use its native language and the discontent will pass of itself. A minority is discontented not because there is no artificial union but because it does not possess its own schools. Give it its own schools and all grounds for discontent will disappear. (Stalin, 1913, *Works*, Vol. 2, p. 376.)

We shall see that Soviet forms give none of the realities of autonomy to the peoples concerned. It now appears that this was not originally due to some Machiavellian cunning but that the Communists really believed that national aspirations would be satisfied by certain minimal concessions.

As to the actual form of the state in multinational Russia, the original view of the Bolsheviks was hostile to a federal solution. Lenin stated in 1913:

> Federation means a union of equals depending upon consent. . . . We reject federation on principle; it weakens economic links; it is an unsuitable form for our State. (Lenin: *Works*, Vol. 19, p. 453.)

This is, of course, contrary to the later development of the Soviet Constitution, in which the 'Union' republics are, formally speaking, given the right to secede.

Stalin gave the following very illuminating reasons for the apparent revision of policy:

> *First*, the fact that at the time of the October Revolution a number of the nationalities of Russia were actually in a state of complete secession and complete isolation from one another, and, in view of this, federation represented a step forward from the division of the working masses of these nationalities to their closer union, their amalgamation.
> *Secondly*, the fact that the very forms of federation which suggested themselves in the course of Soviet development proved

by no means so contradictory to the aim of closer economic unity between the working masses of the nationalities of Russia as might have appeared formerly, and even did not contradict this aim at all, as was subsequently demonstrated in practice.

Thirdly, the fact that the national movement had proved to be far more weighty a factor and the process of amalgamation of nations far more complicated than might have appeared formerly, in the period prior to the war, or in the period prior to the October Revolution. (Stalin: *Works*, Vol. 13, pp. 32–3.)

The second point, that the *forms* of federation may be combined with the actuality of centralization, is particularly significant.

The U.S.S.R. was now formed from four theoretically independent States — the R.S.F.S.R., the Ukraine, Byelorussia and the Transcaucasian Federation — to which it had been hoped to join at least a Soviet Poland and Latvia, and possibly a whole string of European states. The incorporation of the latter was seen to require a solution even looser in appearance than federation. Stalin wrote to Lenin:

Let us assume the future existence of a Soviet Germany, a Soviet Poland, a Soviet Hungary or a Soviet Finland; these nations which had their own state and their own army . . . will, even as Soviet States, hardly agree to enter into an immediate federation with Soviet Russia after the manner of the Bashkirs or Ukrainians. (Letter of Stalin to Lenin of June 12th, 1920. Not contained in Stalin's *Collected Works*, but found in Lenin's *Collected Works* in the unexpurgated third edition, (Russian) 1932, Vol. 25, p. 624.)

What had happened in several years of revolutionary experience was that the Bolsheviks had discovered that national feeling was too strong to make bare-faced centralization feasible, but that there was a possibility of utilizing constitutional forms of extremely liberal appearance, while preserving the substance of control intact through extra-constitutional apparatus.

Stalin had already reconciled the contradiction between the Communist general emancipatory programme and the practice of forced unity as follows:

Thus, our views on the national question can be reduced to the following propositions:

(a) Recognition of the right of nations to secession;

(b) Regional autonomy for nations remaining with the given State;

(c) Special legislation guaranteeing freedom of development for national minorities;

(d) A single, indivisible proletarian collective, a single party. . . .

It would be impermissible to confuse the question of the *right* of nations freely to secede with the question of whether a nation must *necessarily* secede at any given moment. This latter question must be settled quite separately by the party of the proletariat in each particular case, according to the circumstances. Thus we are at liberty to agitate for or against secession in accordance with the interests of the proletariat, of the proletarian revolution. (Stalin, *Marxism and the National and Colonial Question*.)

It was his point (d) which was decisive.

Even before the formation of the U.S.S.R., when the Ukraine was supposed to be an independent republic, Lenin made a well-known complaint which shows that he did not envisage much local freedom of action and relied on the Party apparatus to prevent it.

The Ukraine is an independent republic. That is very good, but in party matters it sometimes — what is the politest way of saying it? — takes a roundabout course, and we have to get at them somehow, because the people there are sly, and I will not say deceive the Central Committee but somehow or other edge away from us. (Lenin, 1922, *Sochineniya*, 33, p. 267.)

The method of control had already been spelt out bluntly in the Party Programme itself:

The Ukraine, Latvia, Lithuania and Belorussia exist at the present time as separate Soviet republics. Thus is solved for now the question of state structure.

But this does not in the least mean that the Russian Communist Party should, in turn, reorganize itself as a federation of independent Communist Parties.

The Eighth Congress of the R.K.P. resolves: there must exist a *single* centralized Communist Party with a single Central Committee leading all the party work in all sections of the R.S.F.S.R. All decisions of the R.K.P. and its directing organs are unconditionally binding on all branches of the party, regardless of their national composition. The Central Committees of the Ukrainian, Latvian, Lithuanian Communists enjoy the rights of the regional committees of the party, and are entirely subordinated to the Central Committee of the R.K.P. (*Communist Party Programme*, 1918.)

The decision of superior bodies is binding on the parties in the local republics under the Party's present constitution also. Emissaries of the Party Presidium are often sent to carry through reorganizations in the local republics. And the Party has always had an enormous preponderance of Russians — there are more Party members in the Moscow province with its nine million inhabitants than among the whole of the twenty million population of the six Muslim republics, though, indeed, in these latter a high proportion of the membership is Russian too: for instance, at the Uzbek Party Congress in February 1954 there were as many as 189 Russian delegates to 425 Uzbeks (*Pravda Vostoka*, February 17th, 1954).

This has always been the key to Soviet centralism, and the unitary Party's leading role is now even incorporated in Article 126 of the Soviet Constitution. When the original guarantees of autonomy were made, there were local Communists who complained openly that these were meaningless in view of Party centralization.

There are certain key apparatuses, apart from the Party itself, for exercising Moscow control. One is the *Prokuratura*. The Procurator-General of the Union directly appoints the Procurator and his subordinates in all the Union Republics. Their duties are to act as public prosecutors and to check the legality of measures ordered by the authorities of the republics. They have the right to challenge all administrative enactments of these authorities.

In addition (and this is itself enough to render all provisions for autonomy meaningless) it is specifically stated that, unlike other Ministries, 'the M.V.D. of the U.S.S.R. directs the activity of the M.V.D.s of the Union and autonomous republics'. (*Large Soviet Encyclopaedia*, second edition, Vol. 27, 1954.)

The military organization of the U.S.S.R. also ignores the republican layout and the Commanders are almost always as Russian as most of their troops — like Efimov, at present C.-in-C. of the North Caucasus district into which Kalmykia as well as Chechnia and the other mountain nations fall.

At the time when the U.S.S.R. was in the process of formation the Georgian Communist leader, Makharadze stated clearly the contradiction between the centralized reality and the autonomous theory:

> There has been talk here of independent and autonomous republics. On this point it is necessary to exert the greatest caution so as to avoid any kind of exaggeration whatsoever. Comrades, it is clear to all of us, what sort of autonomy, what sort of independence this is. We have, after all, a single Party, a single central organ, which in the final resort determines absolutely everything for all the republics, even for the tiny republics, including general directives right up to the appointment of responsible leaders in this or that republic — all this derives from the one organ so that to speak under these conditions of autonomy, of independence reflects, to the highest degree, an intrinsically incomprehensible proposition. (*Twelfth Congress of the Russian Communist Party (Bolsheviks), Stenographic Report*, Moscow, 1923, p. 472.)

His remarks remain true to this day.

The increased liberality with paper Constitutional arrangements went with the reality of the imposition of the new regime on the border areas by Russian Communists, arms in hand. As foreseen by theory, the rights of the socialist 'big nation' were taken as paramount.

These were put concretely enough by Stalin in 1920 when he said:

> Central Russia, that hearth of world revolution, cannot hold out long without the assistance of the border regions, which abound in raw materials, fuel and foodstuffs. (Stalin, *Works*, Vol. 4, p. 363.)

That Soviet power was alien to these border regions was freely conceded at the time — as again by Stalin when he wrote:

Soviet power is not power divorced from the people; on the contrary it is the only power of its kind, having sprung from the Russian masses and being near and dear to them . . . .

Soviet power must become just as near and dear to the masses of the border regions of Russia. But this requires that it should first of all be comprehensible to them. (Stalin: *Works*, Vol. 4, pp. 270–71.)

An interesting subsidiary argument with a respectable Marxist look has been developed in recent years to justify the setting up of the proletarian dictatorship in countries without a proletariat — such as, in effect, Chechnia. The proletarian dictatorship has been defined as a particular form of alliance between proletariat and peasantry, with the former in actual power. It is now said that the Russian proletariat will serve as an adequate substitute in the case of peasant nations without a proletariat of their own: 'The alliance of the Russian working class with the peasantry of all the nationalities' is the formula put forward in *Kommunist* (October 1953).

(Here it is worth noting that the Soviet theory of the development of primitive peoples directly into 'socialism' has been confused by the first but by no means the last of the pseudo-sciences now incorporated and ossified in orthodox Marxism, the anthropology of the American, Morgan, which Engels brought into the canon in his *Origin of the Family, Private Property and the State* — though, on the whole, this was a fairly harmless aberration, more on the lines of the ridiculous theories of Marr which for so long dominated Soviet linguistics, than actively dangerous and damaging stuff like Lysenko's biology or Zhdanov's aesthetics.)

There have been frequent Soviet admissions that border populations were actually conquered, against their will, by Russian Communist forces. For instance, the first edition of the *Encyclopaedia* says 'During the civil war, the majority of the Buryat-Mongol masses came out against the revolution' (*Large Soviet Encyclopaedia*, 1st edition, Vol. 8). It may be of more significance to see what is still being said:

Detachments of Red Guards, arriving from Central Russia,

helped . . . to smash the bourgeois-nationalist Kokand Autonomous Government. (*Questions of History*, No. 10, 1954, p. 38.)

Without the aid of the Russian working class and the heroic
Red Army the young Soviet power in Turkmenistan and in the
other national border regions unquestionably could not have
overcome all its numerous enemies. (*Kommunist*, No. 6, 1955,
p. 79.)

Even the total absence of local Communists is conceded:

It was necessary sometimes temporarily to make use of known
'fellow-travellers' [poputchiki], because in the first months of the
Soviet regime, in some of the more backward national districts,
there were almost no local Communist cadres. (E. Genkina, *The
Formation of the U.S.S.R.*, p. 3.)

And the rights and wrongs of the matter, from a Soviet view-
point have recently been stated with absolute clarity:

The first Bashkir Congress was called at Orenburg on July
19th, 1917 . . . . The counter-revolutionary slogan 'Bashkiria for
the Bashkirs' was raised. (*Questions of History*, No. 9, 1957.)

From this, the punitive measures taken in the Caucasus and
the Crimea can be seen in perspective. The national rights of
Kalmyk and Chechen do not count in the face of allegedly
higher considerations.

Chapter 9

CONSTITUTIONAL ARRANGEMENTS
AND SOVIET PRACTICE

The constitutional guarantees by which the deported peoples were supposed to have been distinguished from mere subject races such as those of the 'imperialist' powers, had read impressively, and still do. The Soviet Union is now, on paper, a federation of equal republics representing the larger nationalities. The smaller nationalities, too, have autonomous republics and autonomous regions, which form part of the larger republics.

Article 15 of the present Soviet Constitution states: 'The sovereignty of the Union Republics is limited only in the spheres defined in Article 14 of the Constitution'. Article 14, however, reserves to the Central Government the spheres of war and peace, diplomatic relations, defence, foreign trade, State security (which, of course, overrides everything else), changes in the mutual frontiers of Republics, economic planning, credit and currency, education, and many other matters. These reserved powers are so much wider than those contained in any other federal system in the world that the Union Republics are left with no autonomy except in trivialities — and even these are frequently referred to the Central Government.

The Union Republics do not, even as legal fiction, own their own natural resources. The coal, oil, copper and agricultural land are the property of the U.S.S.R. as a whole.

The influence of the smaller nations in the allegedly 'highest organ of State power', the Supreme Soviet of the U.S.S.R., is appropriately small. In the Soviet of the Union representation is on a population basis. The disadvantage to the minor nationalities of this is said to be counterbalanced by the existence of the Soviet of Nationalities, a house having supposedly equal powers with the Soviet of the Union. But here, too, there has been a tendency to discriminate against the smaller nations. Thus, whereas in the original 1923 Constitution of the U.S.S.R. five representatives were allowed for each Union Republic and five for each Autonomous Republic in the Soviet of Nationalities, the proportion is now twenty-five to eleven. Nor are all of these deputies local nationals. For instance of the twenty deputies to both Chambers from Bashkiria, only eight are Bashkirs or Tatars. Moreover there are a number of points which make even these provisions worthless. Elections are not contested and only persons approved by the centralized Communist Party are eligible. (The farcical nature of these elections is well demonstrated by the fact that the Volga Germans are said to have given a 99·7 per cent vote to the Government list in 1938.) And republics are abolished and their representatives removed simply by governmental order.

Moreover the value of the representation of the minorities in the Supreme Soviet naturally depends on the powers of that body. Theoretically it is the supreme organ of government. But the fact that the Party, and in practice the Party leadership, holds the realities of rule is admitted even in the constitution. And we find that when a government decree requires to be given special authority this is provided by putting it out jointly in the name of the Council of Ministers and the Central Committee of the Party. The justification of this practice is made clear enough in a political work published by the U.S.S.R. Academy of Science:

> In particular, specially important cases, where questions of great political importance are being settled, joint decrees of the Council of Ministers (formerly the Council of People's Commissars of the U.S.S.R.) and of the Central Committee of the All-Union Communist Party (Bolsheviks) are issued. The decrees

of the Government in such cases acquire the significance of Party directives. The Government act is provided then with the whole strength of the prestige enjoyed by the leading organ of the Party. (*The Theory of State and Law*, Moscow, 1949, p. 380.)

This was written before Stalin's death. But in recent years Party powers have actually increased, and the signature to joint decrees now lists the Party Central Committee before the Government, as was not the case in Stalin's time.

The Supreme Soviet is supposed to have the powers of a Western parliament. The length of its sessions indicates some of the actual difference. In 1955 it sat for fourteen days; in 1956 for five and in 1957 for fifteen. In between times it is represented by its Presidium which issues decrees later ratified by the Supreme Soviet itself. And even the Presidium is simply a ratifying body to decisions of the Party. This was shown, for example, in the expulsion of Malenkov, Molotov and the 'anti-Party group' from the Central Committee in June 1957. This was followed instantly by their dismissal from their government posts by a decree of the Presidium of the Supreme Soviet, only ratified by the Supreme Soviet proper on December 20th. There has never been an instance of the Supreme Soviet rejecting any decree issued by this presidium.

In 1957 the main annual session of the Supreme Soviet lasted from February 5th to February 12th. On February 5th the report on by-elections and the agenda were laid before both chambers and adopted unanimously. On February 6th–9th both chambers adopted the — highly controversial — economic measures, then at issue, including the state plan and the budget. There were thirty-two speeches in the Soviet of Nationalities, and the plan and budget were approved unanimously. Seven more resolutions and legislative proposals of some importance were adopted between February 9th and the end of the session. Twenty-one more speeches were made in the Soviet of Nationalities and all proposals were adopted unanimously. None of the speakers in any of these debates introduced a critical note. On the contrary, the speeches gave the impression of being complementary, each presenting some particular aspect of the Party's proposals. Foreign affairs, for example, might have been expected to have aroused some qualms about official policy in view of the events in Eastern Europe over the previous months. In fact only eleven speeches were made, as unanimously favourable as the vote itself.

It can be deduced that the constitutional arrangements of the U.S.S.R. are not, at present, of the slightest real significance. We should seek the realities of rule and of policy elsewhere.

That Soviet practice is more in accord with the theoretical views laid down by Lenin and Stalin and accepted to this day, has been demonstrated strikingly enough by the events described in the earlier chapters of this book. A few other aspects of this side of Soviet reality need to be considered briefly, simply to sketch in the background as a whole. For thorough treatment the reader is referred to such works as Mr. Kolarz's *Russia and Her Colonies*.

After the formation of the U.S.S.R., things settled down, and such formal changes as have since taken place are of minor importance. In practice, though, a considerable evolution has come about. This we have already seen demonstrated in the case of the Chechens and others, whose national feelings were at first allowed a measure of expression and whose history was at first treated sympathetically, with the gradual change to the imposition of active subservience, even in words, to Russia proper.

The central theme of Soviet policy towards the smaller nations of the Union was expressed succinctly by Kalinin thus:

> The aim of Soviet policy has always been to teach the people of the Kirghiz steppe, the small Uzbek cotton grower, and the Turkmenian gardener to accept the ideals of the Leningrad worker. (M. Kalinin, *During these Years*, Moscow, 1929, Vol. 3, p. 385.)

If this is taken sociologically we may consider it as merely indicating the proletarianization of national cultures — a sort of first step towards that dissolution of national peculiarities which Lenin foresaw. But during the process of the imposition of the ideals of the Russian worker the fact of his being Russian began to count as much as, and then more than his working class status. For national feelings exist to be utilized, in the Communist view, and when it became apparent that local nationalism was far stronger and more persistent than the Communist leaders had hoped, it was natural enough to counter it with the one national feeling which favoured the large centralized industrialized state: that of the Great Russians. In a general way this fusion of claims for the Russian nation into 'Soviet patriotism' produced a curious chauvinism *vis-à-vis* the outer world — showing itself absurdly in such things as claims to have invented everything and so on. Internally it resulted in a high-pressure campaign to rewrite local history in order to prove that Tsarist annexation had been a good thing, the imposition of the Cyrillic alphabet, and the forced introduction of Russian words into local vocabularies. Local writers produced eulogies of Russia. Indeed the present 'national' anthems of the republic (for instance those of Azerbaijan and Kazakhstan) actually contain expressions of gratitude to the Russians. The extremes of Russification have been moderated since Stalin's death, but only to an extent. And the official view is still as stated in *The Short Philosophical Dictionary* (Moscow, 1955) that 'the peoples of the U.S.S.R. rallied round the Great Russian people, who represent the most outstanding nation of all the nations that form part of the Soviet Union'. And in the international sphere it is at least interesting that the conference of Communist Parties held in Moscow in November 1957 spoke of the necessity of having a 'leading nation' in the movement: the U.S.S.R.

That nationality is a phenomenon of the capitalist period and that the interests of the large Communist state must prevail, had as a corollary the view that anyone within the U.S.S.R. who spoke for the rights, or even for the genuine history, of a minority people was not only a nationalist but a 'bourgeois nationalist'. Indeed, the words are inseparable in all Soviet remarks about nationalism. This resulted in a series of purges which are still going on. A whole series of Communist leaders fell in the thirties — including practically all the local prime ministers, presidents and secretaries of the Communist Party. (In the Ukraine three prime ministers went in a year.) One of the few who had a public trial was Khodzhayev, Prime Minister of Uzbekistan, who confessed, amongst other things, to have 'planned to develop industry . . . in such a way as to be more economically independent . . . of the Soviet Union'. At the same time that the political leaders fell all the cultural institutions were purged.

If we look at the map of the Communist world we see a number of rather curious things about it. In principle the proponents of world socialism, including Marx, have thought either in terms of a world state or of a federation in which component states are provided for every important nation. We see, on the contrary, two great empires with a frontier between them that was accidentally reached on a power basis by their imperialist predecessors. Moreover, these frontiers partition big nations. If there can be a Communist Russia and a Communist China one might ask why there could not be a Communist Turkestan. Instead the Turki peoples of the area are divided into two — even using different alphabets. For the huge area inhabited by Mongols it is worse still. They are partitioned into three separate states: an autonomous republic in the U.S.S.R., a 'People's Republic', and an 'autonomous area' in China. The temporarily independent states of the Caucasus were forced into the Soviet Union and the Baltic States, after a much longer period of independence, were also annexed.

In foreign policy the Soviet view of the overriding interests of the larger state were expressed in the Nazi Soviet Pact which spoke of the 'State interests' of the two powers over the territories of Poland and the Baltic States, then independent countries. In fact there was a curious piece of dickering whereby the German claim to Lithuania was sold to the Russians for a slice of Poland and some money compensation. At the same time there was a lot of discussion as to where the Soviet sphere of influence in Asia should be, Molotov claiming expansion southwards 'in the direction of the Persian Gulf'. (The annexation of the Baltic States was in violation of treaties 'renouncing all rights of sovereignty for ever', a non-aggression pact and convention defining aggression, and mutual assistance pacts signed in 1939.)

There is another widespread phenomenon in Soviet Asia, which is particularly germane to the areas of the deported nations. That is, the influx of Russian and Ukrainian settlers. In Kazakhstan and Kirgizia, where the local nationalities were well in the majority in the twenties, they were already barely holding their own by the end of the thirties, and the new influx into the 'Virgin Lands' initiated by Khrushchev in 1954 has further affected the position. The elections to the Kazakh Supreme Soviet — the showpiece of local autonomy — in March 1955, produced 220 European delegates to 201 Central Asians (and 3 Koreans). Russian influence in the Party (whose local First Secretary is the Russian Belyaev), the State, the Police and Industry is very much greater than this.

If this goes much further it may even lead to the official down-grading of the Kazakh S.S.R. The Karelo-Finnish S.S.R. was recently reduced to an A.S.S.R. on the grounds that its population was now largely Russian. But the real importance of this incident is not with the formalities of the matter. It indicates that a Union Republic, let alone an autonomous one, cannot complain about being swamped by Russian immigrants. If we consider the case of the returning Chechens, it seems plain that the implication about not upsetting the economic interests of the Russian settlers who have taken their lands (see p. 135) may well mean that no withdrawal is contemplated at all, and the Chechens will have to make do as best they can, like the Kazakhs.

A further aspect of Soviet policy in this matter is the use of the most Russianized towns available for the capitals of the various republics. Baku in Azerbaijan, Frunze in Kirghizia, Stalinabad in Tadzhikistan, Makhach Kala in Daghestan, are towns with a very high proportion of Russian inhabitants. Grozny, capital of Chechniya, and Petrozavodsk, capital of Karelia, are Russian towns with Russian names. In some cases capitals have been transferred to suit this tendency — the Uzbek capital was moved from Samarkand to semi-European Tashkent in 1930, and the Volga-German capital from Markstadt to the Slav Pokrovsk in 1922; and, to take a smaller territory, the administration of the Udmurt Autonomous Province was moved from the traditional capital of Glasov to the old Russian industrial town of Izhevsk.

That economic development of a backward area need not necessarily confer any blessings on the local population is admitted in Soviet writings; it may be carried out by a big Power for 'selfish motives,' and constitute 'an encroachment on the national sovereignty of the recipient country'. (Academician E. Zhukov in the Soviet English-language magazine *News*, March 1956.)

This particular argument was, of course, used of Britain and France. Yet it remains to be proved that Soviet economic rule has brought particular benefits. In certain cases it clearly has not. According to *Questions of History* (October 1955) 'The present-day Khakassians living in the Khakassian Autonomous Province are a minority in the national composition of Khakassia. The non-Khakassian population of Khakassia forms a majority and outnumbers the Khakassians several times. This has occurred during the last 20 years chiefly because the Khakassians, few in number, were not in a position to ensure the rapid development of a powerful industry having All-Union and All-State importance, for the establishment of which favourable local conditions exist. This circumstance brought about a great influx of non-Khakassians, principally Russians, into Khakassia. The few Khakassians found themselves interspersed among a non-Khakassian majority . . . The percentage of Khakassians in the population of the towns of Abakan [the capital], Chernogorsk and the workers' settlements of Khakassia is quite insignificant . . . What has been said of the Khakassians is also applicable to the Shors of Kemerovo Province . . . and the Altais of the High Altai Autonomous Province . . . It is difficult to say what will be the ultimate fate of each of the small ethnographic groups and peoples . . .'

It is in the linguistic and cultural field that it is sometimes claimed, even by those who realize its political insignificance, that the Soviet idea of autonomy gives results. The figures are not available for the newly repatriated nations but, among their neighbours, the following percentages of pupils receive their education in the native tongue:

Kabardine-Balkar A.S.S.R. -	24%	(in Kabardinian)
Adygei Autonomous Province -	11%	(in Adygei)
Karachai-Cherkess Autonomous		
Province - - - -	9%	(in Circassian)
North Ossetian A.S.S.R. - -	19%	(in Ossetian)

(*Kulturnoe Stroitelstvo*, Moscow, 1958)

We may thus summarize the whole Soviet position on nationality as follows. Communist theory presents the national question as secondary and ephemeral. National interests are to be sacrificed where necessary to the interests of the proletarian revolution. These are normally to be identified with the interests of large Communist nations.

Nevertheless, national sentiment must be 'utilized' where possible. And in multinational Communist states constitutional arrangements should be made which give every apparent concession to local feeling that does not affect the substance of centralized control. The formula used — 'national in form, Socialist in context' — may be interpreted as 'loyalty to the large Communist nation expressed in the language of the small nation'. The constitutional arrangements, formally interpreted, might seem to contradict the theory behind the Communist attitude. But practice is, in reality, completely in accord with theory.

All the same practical policy may vary. Though the leadership remains united on the central issue of never granting the substance of autonomy, there may be divergencies about how much even of the shadow to grant. For to talk too much about a minority's freedom or its revolutionary past, may (and does) encourage thoughts of real freedom and of a revolutionary future. On the other hand to suppress all this and insist on overt obeisance to all things Russian may (and does) produce resentment of an equally nationalist character. There are also, in extreme cases of repression like the deportations, considerations of the propaganda effect in non-Communist countries.

Of the post-Stalin leadership it was Beria who became most closely identified with a policy of greater concessions to the smaller nationalities of the Soviet Union. He reinstated, in Georgia, a number of leaders who had been 'victims' of 'a provocative affair concerning a non-existent nationalism', and arrested or degraded their persecutors. When he himself fell he was charged, among other things, with

> a number of criminal measures to step up the activity of the remnant of bourgeois-nationalist elements in the Union Republics, to sow enmity and discord between the peoples of the U.S.S.R. and, in the first place, to undermine the friendship of the peoples of the U.S.S.R. with the Great Russian people.

A few weeks before the coup against Beria, L. G. Melnikov, First Secretary of the Ukrainian Communist Party and a candidate member of the Party Presidium of the C.P.S.U., was dismissed from all his posts for 'distortions' and 'gross errors' of a Russifying type in 'carrying out the nationality policy of the Party'. Though Beria seems to have made the running in this case (and Meshik, his then representative in the Ukraine, was later shot with him) he could scarcely have brought down this important figure without the support or acquiescence of the other members of the Presidium. Nor, when Beria fell, was Melnikov fully reinstated. It is true that he did then get another post — as Ambassador in Rumania, but he has never been restored even to full membership of the Central Committee (although he again became a minister and later was sent as economic boss of Kazakhstan, a significant post for a notorious Russifier, especially in connection with the influx of Russians in the Virgin Lands campaign. There he was severely censured and 'punished' for economic malpractices in 1958, apparently as an example to others.)

This, and other considerations, seem to show that though the Presidium majority condemned Beria's concessions to national feeling, they did not favour, either, the other extreme of naked Russian domination — Stalin's policy. And this willingness to concede more of the appearance, if not much in the way of substance, has been a fairly constant attitude of the regime though all the post-Beria years. The present attitude to Shamil, gone into in Chapter 11, is a fair indication of the position. The rehabilitation of the deported peoples was the last and most important move in the abandonment of naked aggression against the nationalities. And the position is now roughly what it was in the mid-Stalin period — after he had fully established the primacy of the Russians, but before he had laid down their right to dominate entirely. 'Bougeois national-ism' remains the great enemy. But it is no longer to be com-bated by repression alone.

Khrushchev had been prominent in purging the Ukraine of the mildest signs of nationalism in the period of the Yezhov terror. But in 1947 the vagaries of the struggle for power put him in a position where he had to defend a slightly more moderate position on nationalism than that of his opponents. He was under pressure for his alleged softness to Ukrainian nationalism, when Kaganovich was sent to take his place as First Secretary in the Ukraine, with orders to put down separatist manifestations in literature and elsewhere. (He described this episode in 1957, while attacking Kaganovich in connection with the purge of the 'Anti-Party Group'.) He had survived this, and regained his position at the end of the same year, so that Stalin's suspicions cannot have been very solidly based. But the one significant change Khrushchev has made since his coming to power is a tendency to treat the Ukrainians, with the Russians, as first-class citizens — though Ukrainian nationalism continues to be rebuked, and there are occasional executions of members of 'fascist' chauvinist groups. The concessions to the Ukrainians (which include the handing over by the R.S.F.S.R. to the Ukraine of the Crimea, the rightful property of neither) have some resemblance to the *Ausgleich* by which the Austrian was converted into the Austro-Hungarian Empire. They have not reached that stage yet (at present it might be more correct to think of the Russians as first-class citizens, the Ukrainians as second-class, and the remainder as third-class). But if they do it is not likely to be of much benefit to the other Soviet peoples, any more than the Czechs or Croats benefited from the earlier *Ausgleich*. For the present, Ukrainian dislike of Soviet rule seems as intense as anybody's. And one of the main practical effects of the new policy has been that Ukrainians are expected to join in the Russian influx now swamping Kazakhstan and other parts of Central Asia (in the course of which they themselves tend to become Russified, owing to no longer being in compact national areas). The other sphere in which Ukrainians are now seen much more often than before is in the Party and State apparatus in Moscow and throughout the Russian provinces. This, of course, simply means that Khrushchev is using the cadres built up in his old-established Ukrainian fief to serve him in his new and wider empire. These *apparatchiks* are in any case largely denationalized and though the phenomenon may have its effect on Ukrainian national pride, it amounts to little more than the substitution of the Ukraine for Stalin's Georgia as most favoured subject area.

There has, indeed, been a considerable degree of decentralization in recent years, particularly in economic affairs. Khrushchev's own position, officially at least, is now in favour of greater freedom of action at a local level than was the case in Stalin's time. It is, however, freedom of action for the local Party organization, rather than any national concession, and even then it seems to be more a question of economic tactics than of politics. An army is not necessarily less rigidly disciplined because its divisional or brigade commanders are expected to exercise more initiative than in other armies. But in principle, and politically, the system of autonomy in the Soviet Union remains the same as in Stalin's day. As to the basic theory about the treatment of nations there has been no revision. More attention is now paid to that part of Soviet nationality theory which is concerned with providing the appearance of self-rule and preventing nationalism by the concessional aspect of policy. But the concessions are still made within the old basic limits. And it seems sufficiently clear that this side of Soviet nationalities policy is quite simply a façade. That façade had lost a good deal of its usefulness, particularly in impressing the nations of non-Soviet Asia, and it has now been refurnished and repainted. But the essential structure beneath it remains the same.

Taken at its most abstract there is at least something to be said for the Soviet theory. On a very long-term view it may well be possible to look on nationality and national feeling as temporary phenomena, and to envisage the rise of a world language and a world culture in which the best of present national cultures is subsumed, at least to an extent. In a few thousand years, indeed, such changes might well be expected to occur. But, just the same, to look forward to that and to attempt to force them, to regard such things as having anything whatever to do with immediate issues is a little peculiar. Such developments could only be long, spontaneous and taking place in ways which we are unable to foresee, let alone compel.

It is also true that the extremes of nationalism produce unworthy results, and that some form of loyalty to an overriding conception of mankind as a whole is praiseworthy. Yet here the Soviet theorists seem to combine the worst of both worlds. They all acclaim the nationalisms which they hope to use politically against their opponents and they suppress local nationalisms of which they disapprove — and not, in practice, in favour of the world as a whole, but in favour of 'Soviet patriotism', a larger but not for that reason more reputable insularity than those of the smaller peoples. And even if largeness were a virtue it is only this one largeness which is permitted — the natural solidarities of the Turkic or Mongol peoples are disrupted rather than encouraged.

For, in the first place the Soviet attitude is cynical: it wishes to exploit or delude those who feel national sentiments. And secondly, like all such cynicisms, this has led to obtuseness: the Soviet leaders have misunderstood and underestimated the power of feelings which are outside their own experience. The result has been shallow calculations, and these have not

worked. National feeling has remained unsatisfied in the
U.S.S.R. After twenty years of empty phrases the Chechens
showed that for them the realities had never been obscured.
After thirty-five years, the nationalist students of favoured
Georgia demonstrated in the streets of their capital.

At the very time when the rehabilitations were proceeding
various pronouncements made it clear that nationalism is
recognized to be, still, a major and undying danger. The
Secretary of the Communist Party of Armenia, B. Sarkisov (in
an article in *Party Life*, No. 8, 1957), warned against new and
'subtle' ideological arguments of the nationalists. A report in
Komsomolskaya Pravda (April 24th, 1957) of a session of the
Komsomol Central Committee in Estonia carried warnings in
similar terms. Some of the deputies from border republics in
the Supreme Soviet of the U.S.S.R. also referred at this time
to the dangers of the new nationalist propaganda. And so it
has gone on.

A speech by Mukhitdinov, member of the Party Presidium,
and Khrushchev's protégé, at an All-Union Conference of
Orientalists, held in Tashkent in June 1957, is particularly
authoritative. He found it necessary to say,

> In all its successes the Uzbek people, like people of other
> national republics, is indebted to its own Soviet regime and the
> Communist Party, to friendship between peoples, their fraternal
> mutual aid and in the first place to the aid of the great Russian
> people. For example, could the Uzbek people alone, outside the
> family of Soviet peoples and without the aid of the great Russian
> people, really face the onslaught of foreign interventionists,
> internal counter-revolution and the Basmachestvo and retain
> their independence? Could the Uzbek people alone, without the
> aid of other peoples, really make the leap from ancient backward-
> ness to socialism and by-passing the agonizing stage of capitalism
> create in a short space of time a powerful industry and advanced
> socialist agriculture, equipped with modern techniques? Could
> the Uzbek people, before the revolution almost completely
> illiterate, really carry out without the aid of other peoples of the
> Soviet Union a cultural revolution, and develop cadres of their
> own national intelligentsia? Of course not! We are proud of the
> brotherhood and friendship of the great Russian and other
> peoples of our country.

Mukhitdinov added that they would never be reconciled with survivals of nationalism in whatever form they appeared, and went on:

> Nationalism in our country has not now a social, class basis, but nationalistic survivals can still appear in the activities of individual persons in the most varied forms, in particular in the idealization of the feudal past, a scornful and haughty attitude to the traditions, culture, and language of other peoples, especially small peoples, in the lack of understanding of the international duty of its people, in the aspiration to belittle the great aid rendered by other peoples to the Uzbek people, and in other most varied forms. . . . We must further intensify the struggle against manifestations in any form of survivals of great power chauvinism and local nationalism. (*Pravda Vostoka*, June 13th, 1957.)

We may conclude with a recent statement of interest in both practice and theory in which a leading Soviet theoretical journal reaffirms the applicability of an early and blunt declaration of Lenin's:

> Some theoreticians who consider themselves to be internationalists, limit their internationalism merely to the recognition of the equality of rights of nations. But such 'internationalism' fits in completely with bourgeois and petty bourgeois nationalism as it fails to rise to the heights of proletarian internationalism. Lenin wrote: 'Petty bourgeois nationalism declares that internationalism is a recognition of the equality of the rights of nations and nothing more, retaining national egoism untouched (without speaking about the purely verbal character of such a recognition), whereas proletarian internationalism demands first and foremost a subordination of the interests of the proletarian fight in one country to the interests of that fight on a worldwide scale; and secondly it demands the ability and the readiness of a nation which has won victory over the bourgeoisie to go to the length of the most extreme national sacrifices for the sake of the over-throw of international capital. (*Works*, Vol. 5, 31, p. 126.) (*Questions of Philosophy*, No. 1, 1957.)

Thus, still, in the international sphere as much as within the Soviet Union, all considerations are subordinated to the total triumph of a group of rulers claiming to represent, in a round-about fashion, the supposed interests of a world proletariat. They have learnt nothing and forgotten nothing. Or very little.

Chapter 10

REAPPEARANCE AND
REHABILITATION FOR SOME

The decade of silence about the deportees was broken in 1955, with the first of a number of very slight and unimportant references which yet conceded the existence of some of these peoples, and at the same time revealed officially, for the first time, some of their new locations.

The first announcement seems to have been this note in *Kazakhstanskaya Pravda* of May 17th, 1955:

> Subscription is invited for the second half-year of 1955 for a republican weekly paper 'Kinghegaman Bairakh' [Banner of Labour] published in the Chechen language. The subscription rate for 6 months is 10 roubles, 40 kopeks. Subscriptions are accepted by town departments of Soyuzpechat [Press Union] and by district offices, by communications agencies and offices, and also at points for accepting subscriptions in undertakings, collective farms, State farms and machine tractor stations.

Simply as a public reference to the Chechens, this was a step forward, though the provision of the paper itself is of no special importance: for the authorities provide propaganda sheets and lectures even in the labour camps themselves.

At first even such references were few and far between. There was a report in *Sotsialisticheski Kazakhstan* of November 27th, 1955 about a Chechen-Ingush art theatre, which again marks a further advance. But at some point about now the decision must have been taken to rehabilitate most of the deported nations. For the announcement that they had been wronged was made in Khrushchev's Secret Speech of February 1956 at the Twentieth Party Congress. This was, indeed, confidential; yet its contents became widely known in the U.S.S.R. That it did not produce legislative results for nearly a year is a little curious, but in any case it certainly represented a new and less repressive approach on the part of the Soviet leaders who had hitherto been content to follow Stalin's policies.

At the Congress it had also been made clear that the deportees did not, so far, have the normal political rights of other Soviet nations. Aristov, Secretary of the Central Committee reporting for the Credentials Committee on February 16th, 1956, stated that delegates to the Congress had been elected from among a list of nationalities going down as low as ones as small as the Udmurts, Ossetians, Komis, Yakuts and Maris. None of the purged nations was mentioned.

Khrushchev's speech, which will be looked at later, named only the Chechens, Ingushi, Balkars, Karachai and Kalmyks as suffering peoples, making no reference to the Volga Germans or Crimean Tatars. And it was of the first group only that reports were now appearing — except that nothing seems to have been said of the Kalmyks.

A further indication appeared during 1956. A *Collection of Laws of the Supreme Soviet and Decrees of the Presidium of the Supreme Soviet 1938 — July 1956* came out — passed for publication on August 27th, 1956. It quoted only a few decrees having a bearing on the deported nations: a decree of September 7th, 1941, partitioning the Volga German Republic between Saratov and Stalingrad Provinces, and a decree of June 30th, 1945, transforming the Crimean A.S.S.R. into the Crimean Province. That is, decisions involving the republics *not* selected for rehabilitation in the Secret Speech. Otherwise there was only one relevant decree: one of March 22nd, 1944, on the 'creation of Grozny Province with centre at Grozny, and liquidation in this connection of the Grozny and Kizlyar Okrugs of the Stavropol Territory', naming the raions of the abolished Okrugs (and one from Stavropol), which were to enter the new unit. Thus a reorganization of the first (hitherto unknown) post-Chechen administrative arrangements was

K

published, but not any of the decrees actually dealing with the end of the autonomy of the Chechens — or any others of those now to be rehabilitated.

Not that the attempts at reconciliation, even with those mentionable, were going as well as all that. *Sovietskaya Kirghizia* (February 11th, 1956) revealing the presence of Chechens in the Kalininskoye area, complained of a lack of 'cultural and educational work among the Chechen population, a considerable number of whom still retain feudal and ancestral survivals'. The paper added that there had been no lectures at all given in Chechen over the past year.

But now other deported nations had begun to reappear. They too were in localities where unofficial reports had already placed them. *Kazakhstanskaya Pravda* of April 15th, 1956, announced that the Party town committee in Kokchetav (North Kazakhstan) had organized a group of lecturers to give talks on the Twentieth Congress in the Ingush language. *Sovietskaya Kirghizia* of May 19th, 1956, announced that the Kirghiz State Publishing House 'has begun to publish the works of Karachai-Balkarian writers in their native languages'. An anthology included poems by leading Karachai-Balkar poets on 'Lenin; the heroic feats of the peoples of the U.S.S.R. in the great patriotic war; and the struggle for peace'. All these subjects, and in particular the second one, might be thought of as ones which the peoples concerned have little reason to be lyrical about. Then Chechens and Ingushi — 'farm workers' — were reported in the Bulaevsk raion, in the extreme north of Kazakhstan (*Kazakhstanskaya Pravda*, July 4th, 1956).

Right up to the official announcement of the rehabilitations, these references remained sporadic. For instance, Alma Ata Radio of December 18th, 1956, stated that in 1957 the Kazakh State Literary Publishing House would produce works in Russian, Kazakh, Uighur, Chechen and Ingush. The same station reported a Karachai-Balkar dance ensemble in the city on January 20th, 1957. But little more than these cultural hints appeared.

Khrushchev had clearly implied that the whole deportation

was a crime and should be reversed. What he said on the matter in the Secret Speech was:

Comrades, let us reach for some other facts. The Soviet Union is justly considered as a model of a multi-national state because we have in practice assured the equality and friendship of all nations which live in our great fatherland.

All the more monstrous are the acts whose initiator was Stalin and which are crude violations of the basic Leninist principles of the nationality policy of the Soviet State. We refer to the mass deportations from their native places of whole nations, together with all Communists and Komsomols without any exception; this deportation action was not dictated by any military considerations.

Thus, already at the end of 1943, when there occurred a permanent break-through at the fronts of the great patriotic war in favour of the Soviet Union, a decision was taken and executed concerning the deportation of all the Karachai from the lands on which they lived. In the same period, at the end of December 1943, the same lot befell the whole population of the Autonomous Kalmyk Republic. In March 1944 all the Chechen and Ingush people were deported and the Chechen-Ingush Autonomous Republic was liquidated.

In April 1944, all Balkars were deported to faraway places from the territory of the Kabardine-Balkar Autonomous Republic and the Republic itself was renamed Autonomous Kabardine Republic. The Ukrainians avoided meeting this fate only because there were too many of them and there was no place to which to deport them. Otherwise, he would have deported them also. (Laughter and animation in the hall.)

Not only a Marxist-Leninist but also no man of common sense can grasp how it is possible to make whole nations responsible for inimical activity, including women, children, old people, Communists and Komsomols, to use mass repression against them, and to expose them to misery and suffering for the hostile acts of individual persons or groups of persons.

This statement made certain points clear. It confirmed, approximately, the dates of the deportations — giving, in addition, the Balkar date, hitherto unknown. It confirmed that some hostile activity had taken place. And it exposed the rather perfunctory attempt of the earlier decrees to imply that the work was simply a humane resettlement, by its reference to 'misery and suffering' inflicted.

More important, it foreshadowed an effort to put an end to their sufferings.

REHABILITATION

At the meeting of the Supreme Soviet in February 1957 the rehabilitations finally went through. In his speech Gorkin (who had been a signatory of the original deportation decrees) dealt with the matter in the following terms — worth quoting as the first public statement on the matter ever put before the Soviet peoples:

> By a decree of January 9th, 1957, the Presidium of the Supreme Soviet of the U.S.S.R. recommended the Presidium of the Supreme Soviet of the R.S.F.S.R. to examine the question and take decisions:
> On the reorganization of the Kabardine A.S.S.R. into the Kabardine-Balkar A.S.S.R.,
> On the restoration of the Chechen-Ingush A.S.S.R. in the structure of the R.S.F.S.R.,
> On the formation of the Kalmyk autonomous province in the structure of the R.S.F.S.R.,
> On the reorganization of the Cherkess autonomous province into the Karachai-Cherkess autonomous province.
> In accordance with these decisions the Presidium of the Supreme Soviet of the R.S.F.S.R. passed Decrees on the reorganization of the Kabardine A.S.S.R. into the Kabardine-Balkar A.S.S.R., on the restoration of the Chechen-Ingush A.S.S.R., on the formation of a Kalmyk autonomous province and on the reorganization of the Cherkess autonomous province into the Karachai-Cherkess autonomous province. At the same time the Presidium of the Supreme Soviet of the R.S.F.S.R., for the direction and organization of all work connected with the restoration of autonomies, pending elections of the leading Soviet organs, confirmed organizational committees of representatives of the corresponding nationalities for the Chechen-Ingush A.S.S.R. and the Kalmyk autonomous province.
> Direction of work for the implementation of all measures connected with the reorganization of the Kabardine A.S.S.R. into the Kabardine-Balkar A.S.S.R. and the Cherkess autonomous province into the Karachai-Cherkess autonomous province has been entrusted accordingly to the Council of Ministers of the Kabardine A.S.S.R. and the Executive Committee of the Cherkess

autonomous province, together with representatives of the Balkar and Karachai peoples.

Comrades, deputies! The practical implementation of measures for the restoration of the national autonomy of these peoples requires a certain amount of time and the carrying out of much organizational work in the preparation of the necessary production, housing and other cultural and everyday conditions in places of former residence. Great expenditure of material and monetary funds is also required.

Therefore the resettlement of citizens of the stated nationalities who have expressed the desire to return to regions of former residence must be conducted in an organized manner, in small groups, at definite periods and in order of precedence. These periods and order of precedence, and also all practical questions of labour and everyday arrangements will be determined and solved by organs of State power of the autonomous republics and autonomous provinces being formed.

Such an order will make it possible not to permit certain complications and to avoid difficulties for the population of these nationalities in the matter of labour and living arrangements. It should also be borne in mind that unorganized resettlement can do serious harm to the economy of those collective farms, State farms and enterprises in which workers of these nationalities are employed at the present time. It is therefore necessary to guard against all attempts at unorganized resettlement.

Proceeding from these considerations and bearing in mind the need to prepare in advance conditions of a productive and everyday order it is proposed to conduct the resettlement of citizens of Balkar, Kalmyk and Karachai nationality in the territory of the restored autonomies and organize work for them during 1957 and 1958.

As concerns Chechen and Ingush peoples, as being the most numerous, it is proposed to carry out measures connected with the restoration of their national autonomy over a longer period, between 1957 and 1960.

There is no doubt that republics, territories and provinces on whose territory the Balkars, Chechens, Ingushes, Kalmyks and Karachais are living at the present time will render the necessary assistance in the organized conduct of the resettlement of those desiring to return to their former place of residence, and at the same time will create for those people who continue to live in these republics, territories and provinces, every condition for their active participation in economic and cultural construction together with other peoples of these territories and provinces.

In connexion with the restoration of the Chechen-Ingush A.S.S.R. by a Decree of January 11th, 1957, the Presidium of the Supreme Soviet of the U.S.S.R. has ratified a resolution of the Presidium of the Supreme Soviet of the Georgian S.S.R. and the Presidium of the Supreme Soviet of the R.S.F.S.R. on the handing over of part of the territory of the Dushet and Kazbek regions from the Georgian S.S.R. to the R.S.F.S.R. and on the restoration in such manner of the borders between these union republics which existed up to March 7th, 1944.

In ratifying Decrees on the restoration of the national autonomy of the peoples mentioned it will be necessary to introduce appropriate changes into Article 22 of the Constitution of the U.S.S.R. (*Pravda*, February 12th, 1957.)

Most of this speaks for itself. The date of March 7th, 1944, refers to the then unpublished decree on the destruction and partition of the Chechen-Ingush A.S.S.R., referred to overtly in the 1958 edition of *Administrative Territorial Divisions of the Union Republics* (see p. 140), which may be the rather legalistic reason why Khrushchev gives March, instead of the well-authenticated February, as the date of the Chechen-Ingush deportation. The retrocession of Georgian territory affected only the area annexed from the Chechen-Ingush republic. As far as the territories annexed by Georgia in the Karachai area are concerned, one of the post-rehabilitation volumes of the *Encyclopaedia*, Volume 47, has a short article on the Cherkess Autonomous Province, in which it is said that

the Karachai-Cherkess Autonomous Province was formed on January 9th, 1957, and into it entered the former Cherkess Autonomous Province, the Zelenchuk, Ust-Dzhegntinski and Klukhori Raions of the Stavropol Territory, the rural area of the city of Kislovodsk and the eastern part of the Psebay Raion of the Krasnodar Territory.

Thus even prior to the rehabilitation laws, the Karachai lands formed part of the Stavropol Territory of the R.S.F.S.R. Those which had earlier gone to Georgia had been retroceded to be R.S.F.S.R. by a decree of March 14th, 1955 (*Bulletin of the Supreme Soviet* No. 5 of 1955, quoted in *Collection of Laws of the Soviet Union and Decrees of the Presidium of the Supreme Soviet 1938–1958*). This transfer, of an area which at the time had no expectation of Karachai return, seems to confirm our earlier consideration of the administrative difficulties of the previous arrangement, which had no compensating advantages except in pleasing the Georgians, no longer an important consideration after the deaths of Stalin and Beria.

The law Georgadze proposed was passed in the following form:

Law on confirming the decree of the Presidium of the Supreme Soviet of the U.S.S.R. on the restoration of the national autonomy of the Balkar, Chechen, Ingush, Kalmyk and Karachai peoples.

The Supreme Soviet of the Union of Soviet Socialist Republics decides:

Article 1. To confirm the decrees of the Presidium of the Supreme Soviet of the U.S.S.R. of January 9th, 1957:

On the transformation of the Kabardine A.S.S.R. into the Kabardine-Balkar A.S.S.R.

On the restoration of the Chechen-Ingush A.S.S.R. in the framework of the R.S.F.S.R.

On the formation of a Kalmyk Autonomous Province in the framework of the R.S.F.S.R.

On the transformation of the Cherkess Autonomous Province into the Karachai-Cherkess autonomous province.

Article 2. To confirm the decree of the Presidium of the Supreme Soviet of the U.S.S.R. of January 11th, 1957:

On the transfer of parts of the territories of the Dushet and Kazbek raions from the Georgian S.S.R. to the framework of the R.S.F.S.R.

President of the Presidium of the Supreme Soviet of the U.S.S.R., K. Voroshilov

Secretary of the Presidium of the Supreme Soviet of the U.S.S.R., A. Gorkin

Moscow, Kremlin, February 11th, 1957.

(*Pravda*, February 12th, 1957.)

A further decree of the Supreme Soviet, of February 11th, 1957, runs in part as follows:

Article 2. To delete from Article 22 of the U.S.S.R. Constitution the list of the administrative provinces and territories.

In this connection, and also in connection with the Law 'On the Confirmation of the Decrees of the U.S.S.R. Supreme Soviet Presidium on the Restoration of the National Autonomy of the Balkar, Chechen, Ingush, Kalmyk and Karachai peoples', Article 22 to be read as follows:

Article 22. The R.S.F.S.R. includes the Bashkir, Buryat-Mongolian, Dagestan, Kabarda-Balkar, Karelian, Komi, Mari, Mordovian, North Ossetian, Tatar, Udmurt, Chechen-Ingush, Chuvash and Yakut A.S.S.R.s and of the Adygei, Gorno-Altai, Jewish, Kalmyk, Karachai-Cherkess, Tuva and Khakass Autonomous Provinces.

This completed the promised legislative processes for the moment.

The reduction of the Kalmyks to an Autonomous Province, and the reversion of the Karachai from having an Autonomous Province of their own to sharing one again with their Cherkess neighbours certainly seemed to imply a reduction in their numbers. The precise implications were not entirely clear.

On the one hand propaganda considerations in connection with Soviet influence in Asia, would ordinarily have been expected to produce the maximum effort to keep up the appearance of complete restitution. Unless the populations were very far indeed below the normal minimum one would expect administrative rules or customs to be applied with considerable latitude. In the case of the Kalmyks, for instance, it is known that Asian Governments intervening in favour of fellow Buddhists made several inquiries about their fate. One report says, indeed, that the Soviet authorities stated frankly at some stage that they could not then find more than a few hundred Kalmyks. However that may be, it may be worth looking for something in the way of an upper limit by seeing what populations were usually associated with autonomous provinces and autonomous republics respectively.

I cannot find that it has ever been laid down that a certain population goes with a certain status. On the other hand Kalinin (then President of the U.S.S.R.) promised the Jews that the autonomous province of Birobidzhan which had been allotted to them would be transformed into an autonomous republic, when its Jewish population reached the hundred thousand mark (Kolarz, op. cit., p. 177). This seems to imply that the status depends on the number of the titular nationality in the area, and not the total population. Before the war the Kalmyk Republic was that with the smallest population among the autonomous republics — 220,723. The number of Kalmyks in the Republic was 134,271. The largest autonomous provinces in 1939 had local-nationality populations of 80,000–90,000. The smallest autonomous province was the Cherkess, with about 92,000 inhabitants of which about 65,000 were Cherkess.

If we take these facts, which even if they mean anything can only give us limiting figures, to imply the maximum, rather than the minimum, number of survivors it would not seem unreasonable to make a very rough and speculative guess, that the Karachai may have been reduced to less than 65,000; and also that even with the Cherkess they may not total the minimum required for an A.S.S.R.: that is that 65,000 Cherkess plus Karachai may not number as many as the 130,000 which was the lowest autochthonous population for an A.S.S.R. (this too would mean no more than 65,000 Karachai); and that the Kalmyks may have been reduced from 134,000 to at least not more than *c.* 90,000, the previous number of the local inhabitants of the largest autonomous provinces.

But as we shall see, yet another change was to be made in the Kalmyks' status.

Meanwhile the repudiation of the other official attack on the restored nations followed. An article on 'The Party and Questions of the Development of Soviet Literature and Art' appeared in *Kommunist* of February 1957 (passed for publication February 23rd, 1957). This article, which is a strong justification in principle of the 'Zhdanovist' cultural resolutions of the Central Committee in 1946–8, makes a few reservations. One of these is 'in the resolution on the opera *The Great Friendship* there is a wrong characterization of the Ingush and the Chechens'.

The publication of the rehabilitation decrees in February 1957 was followed by other announcements. For instance there were decrees about reorganization and renaming in the territories concerned.

The *Bulletin of the Supreme Soviet*, No. 8 (875) of April 20th, 1957, publishes a decree of January 12th on changes of name in the Kalmyk Autonomous Province of the Stavropol Territory. The capital, Stepnoi, is changed back to its former Kalmyk name, Elista. Five other villages have changes of name but not obviously significant of de-Russification. (Indeed, one of them actually becomes Komsomolskiy.) The same issue also publishes a decree of January 15th, 1957, on the administrative divisions of the Karachai-Cherkess autonomous province of the Stavropol Territory. Amongst other things the town of Klukhori becomes Karachaevsk.

Administrative Territorial Divisions of the Union Republics (Moscow, 1958) gives some interesting information about the revived republics and provinces. Like the 1941 edition, and unlike those which appeared meanwhile, it gives the populations, though not the proportions of Russian and native inhabitants. These we will consider later.

The Chechen-Ingush A.S.S.R. is given as having an area in 1958 of 19·3 thousand square kilometres as against 15·7 in 1941. The map, though on a small scale, confirms that the republic has gained much territory north of the Terek and lost some in the mountain valleys. It is now formed of seventeen rural districts instead of the twenty-three of its previous organization. Internal reorganization may have taken place (and some centres, such as Sovietskoye, have kept their Russian names) and it appears that three of the new districts are north of the Terek. (The regions of the town of Grozny, incidentally, retain their old names except that the Molotov region has now rather inappropriately been renamed Stalin.) The handbook states that the republic was abolished on March 7th, 1944. This is the first time that a date has been definitely given to this decision, and presumably refers to the decree of the Presidium of the Supreme Soviet whose constitutional confirmation by the Supreme Soviet itself was announced in *Izvestia* more than two years later. It will be noticed that even this

Presidium decree was *ex post facto*, the deportations having actually taken place the previous month.

Of the restored republics the Chechen-Ingush is the only one listed whose dissolution had been previously announced — since the Crimean and Volga German A.S.S.R.s have not been restored. And it is only in connection with the Chechen-Ingush A.S.S.R. that the volume finds it necessary to mention the facts of the dissolution, treating the other revived areas as if they had existed all the time, simply with changes of status. (Why this misleading impression should be given is not really clear even so, for the decree restoring the areas made the whole position public in any case.) The Kalmyk Autonomous Province is given as being very little different in size from the old A.S.S.R. (75·9 thousand square kilometres as against 74·2 in 1941).

On July 29th, 1958, a new decree raising the status of the Kalmyk Autonomous Province once more to that of Autonomous Soviet Socialist Republic was published in the following terms:

> To meet the wishes of the toilers of the Kalmyk Autonomous Province, and being guided by the principles of a free development of nationalities, and in accordance with part *e* of Article 14 of the Constitution of the U.S.S.R., the Presidium of the Supreme Soviet of the U.S.S.R. decrees:
> 1. To confirm the changing of the Kalmyk Autonomous Province into the Kalmyk Autonomous Soviet Socialist Republic, enacted by decree of the Presidium of the Supreme Soviet of the R.S.F.S.R. on July 26th, 1958.
> 2. To submit this decree for confirmation by the Supreme Soviet of the U.S.S.R.
> (Signed)   President: Voroshilov
>   Secretary: Georgadze
> Moscow, Kremlin, July 29th, 1958.

The decisions, first to reduce the Kalmyk territory to an Autonomous Province and then to raise it again to an A.S.S.R., contrast significantly. The natural conclusion from the original rehabilitation decree of January 1957 is that after careful consideration in the year following the statement on the matter in Khrushchev's Secret Speech, it was decided on administrative grounds that the Kalmyks no longer rated a republic. The reason can scarcely have been other than an inadequate population. It hardly seems probable that any new objective factors produced the reconsideration.

At this stage it is unlikely that large numbers of mislaid Kalmyks had after all turned up. Such reports as have been made about Kalmyk resettlement contrast markedly with complaints about the Chechens swarming home prematurely in their hundreds of thousands. In Kalmykia there have been only the barest references to a few hundred here, a few thousand there. For instance, Elista Radio (July 29th, 1957) spoke of the return of 290 families. Even more significantly, Elista Radio on June 12th, 1958, said: *'altogether* 6,000 Kalmyk families are expected to return to the province this year'.

This can hardly mean other than that the total numbers available for repatriation amount to only a few tens of thousands. We shall return to the question of the numbers of survivors later.

If administrative and demographic circumstances have not changed, the motives for the new alteration are presumably to be found on the political and propaganda side. Of all the deported nations, the spokesmen of the Kalmyks in the free world have been most numerous and most effective. They roused the interest of the governments and periodicals of much of Asia, and lobbied effectively at the Cairo and Bandung Conferences. They drew and publicized the obvious conclusion about the demotion to Autonomous Province, and the Soviet leaders may have felt that they had underestimated this point. (In addition, the lowered status implied an admission that the nation had suffered greatly as a result of Stalin's actions: now that the late dictator is in good odour again, arrangements drawing attention to his worst acts may seem less desirable.) In any case, though the practical advantage to the Kalmyks of this particular change is clearly nil, it does perhaps show once more that the Soviet authorities are to some extent influenced by foreign public opinion.

However that may be, the Kalmyks were soon, as if nothing had happened, required to produce the old line in literature. *Literaturnaya Gazeta* of December 29th, 1956, carries an article by N. Narmaev on the revival of Kalmyk-Soviet poetry in which he quotes some Kalmyk poetry of the Stalin period as a model:

> Hearing Lenin's words,
> The Kalmyks took up arms
> Strong and firm in fight
> They won their happiness.

NON-REHABILITATION FOR SOME

With all the restitution that has taken place it cannot fail to be remarked that only two of the four suppressed republics re-emerged. Of the seven deported nations three resumed their old constitutional status. One has been downgraded; and one was downgraded for a time then restored to its old status; and two others, numbering at least 584,000 in 1936, have had no rehabilitation at all.

Quite early on there were references to Germans in Siberia. These may in any given case be the ones settled there already and not the deportees from European Russia. But the whole German minority, even in Siberia, was victimized, and even such reports have some significance. For example, a decree of the Supreme Soviet of April 5th, 1951, making awards to collective farmers, includes a number from farms with German names in the Omsk province (such as *Arbeiter* and *Rosa Luxemburg*).

Other reports almost certainly refer to deportees. For example *Kazakhstanskaya Pravda* of June 7th, 1955, lists the champion dairy-maids of the Republic over the period October 1954 to May 1955. Of the twenty-one names from the Kokchetav, Pavlodar and Semipalatinsk Provinces seventeen are German, while there are four more, apparently German, elsewhere in the Republic, including two out of six names in Karaganda.

Kazakhstanskaya Pravda of June 16th, 1955, gives the champion milk-maids of the State Farms. The German names are one out of three in Kustanai, two out of three in Semipalatinsk, two out of four in South Kazakhstan and two out of two in Kokchetav. These figures probably give a reasonable idea of where the Germans were most highly concentrated in Kazakhstan. They also indicate that the German population on the whole was at least farming under conditions no worse than those of the remainder of the population. In view of the generally superior reputation for livestock and stud-farming of the Soviet Germans, the figures probably should not be thought of as being any indication of the proportion of Germans to the rest of the population. That their civil rights were not, then at least, respected in the same way as their farming abilities, seems clear. A list was published in *Kazakhstanskaya Pravda* of March 11th, 1955, of deputies elected to the Kazakh Supreme Soviet on March 6th, 1955. This list shows three doubtful names: Fedor Efremovich German, Dmitri Ivanovich Berlin and Alexei Andreevich Pak, which may be of German, Jewish or Baltic origin — though Pak is more probably a Korean. (The Christian names are Russian.) Apart from these three doubtfuls there are no Germans among the 425 names listed.

Yet the farm awards showed some progress. And it seems that towards the end of 1955, when the general decision on rehabilitation for the Chechens and others was evidently taken, the Soviet leaders definitely decided to grant a measure of justice to the Germans, though in their case a measure far short of full restitution. No doubt for this reason, the decision has not been given publicly. But a decree of the Presidium of the Supreme Soviet (one of the many which, as we have seen, do not easily reach the public eye) is reported to have appeared in *The Bulletin of Current Legislation of the U.S.S.R.*, No. 5, December 1955 (Moscow, 1956). The original has not been available to me and I quote a text which appeared in the authoritative *Osteuropa-Recht*, No. 1 (July 1958).

Decree of the Presidium of the Supreme Soviet of the U.S.S.R. of December 13th, 1955 — On the Revocation of the Restrictions in the Legal Position of Germans and their family dependents now in conditions of Special Settlement:

Considering the fact that the existing restrictions in the legal position of German special settlers and members of their families, who were deported to various regions of the country, are no longer necessary in future, the Presidium of the Supreme Soviet of the U.S.S.R. decides:

1. Germans and members of their families who at the time of the Great Patriotic War were exiled to a Special Settlement are to be released from attachment to the Special Settlement and freed from the administrative control of the organs of the M.V.D. The same is valid for German citizens of the U.S.S.R. who after their repatriation from Germany were put in a Special Settlement.

2. It is laid down that the revocation of the restrictions on the Germans connected with Special Settlement does not imply the return of the property confiscated in connection with the deportation, and further that they do not have the right to return to the regions from which they were deported.

This throws considerable light on the legal and administrative status of the deported nations at the time of their exile (and the reference to the families, as apart from the Germans themselves, is worth noting, as seeming to imply that non-German wives of Germans suffered the fate of their husbands). On the present limited nature of their rehabilitation, it speaks for itself.

One special effort was made in 1957 to track down a small section of the German minority. These are the Mennonites, a pacifist protestant sect which emigrated from Dutch and Rhineland territories in the eighteenth century, and were, like the other German immigrants, welcomed by the Tsars. Under the Tsars their pacifist principles were respected and they were allowed to join a special forest service instead of serving in the army. At the time of the Revolution there were about 100,000 of them. Among them, owing to their religious principles and practices, there was a total absence of class struggle. Moreover their religion was for them more important than their origins and they protested against inclusion in the 'German National Districts' in the areas where they lived.

Conscientious objection was abolished in Russia in the thirties on the grounds that no-one wished any longer to make such objection. The Mennonites did. The resulting repressive measures were severe, and merged almost imperceptibly, via mass deportations of Mennonite males, into the general removal to Siberia of all the Russian Germans. During the war some contrived to escape through Germany to the West.

In 1957 the Soviet authorities allowed an American, Dr. Binder, and a Canadian, Pastor Wiens, to visit their co-religionists. They searched for them throughout Soviet Asia and finally found rather less than half of the original population. None were in the Ukraine and about half of the survivors were in their old Siberian settlements. The remainder had been resettled, mainly in Kazakhstan and the Altai region. About a thousand of them formed a community in Karaganda, the great exile city in Kazakhstan. Visitors reported that no religious life had been possible for the community for more than twenty years, until 1954, and that they were no longer taught in their own language, so that the younger generation had been considerably Russified.

But some of the same sort of attention had now begun to be paid to the Germans, as targets of political work, as had been the case with the Chechens in 1955–6. *Kazakhstanskaya Pravda* of June 7th, 1957, complained that 'mass political work was especially badly conducted in the native languages among the Uighur, German and Chechen-Ingush nationalities'.

In 1958 two newspapers in German started to appear in the Soviet Union — *Neues Leben* in Moscow and *Arbeit* in Barnaul, capital of the Altai Territory. This seemed to establish that the largest German settlements were in the Altai region though most unofficial reports have referred to areas of the Altai on the steppe fairly distant from Barnaul itself. One of the seventeen German National Districts existing in the U.S.S.R. before the war, over and above the Volga Republic, had been in the Altai. The original circulation announced for *Arbeit* was 6,500 copies. Its treatment of Germans in the U.S.S.R. was, in 1958, rather curious. It described the powers of Soviet tractor drivers and others with German names, but did not refer overtly to the fact of their being German, nor described the happy life of Germans in the U.S.S.R. taken collectively. It also ran a useful and pathetic column through which Germans sought information about members of their families, often last seen fifteen or sixteen years previously. Its existence, and that of *Neues Leben,* is certainly an improvement. But before the war twenty-one German papers came out in the Volga Republic alone.

At the same time German-language broadcasts for Germans in the U.S.S.R. began from Radio Moscow and Radio Alma Ata.

There have been a few references to the Crimean Tatars in the Soviet press — in *Literaturnaya Gazeta, Druzhba Narodov* and elsewhere. Rumours that some have been allowed to return seem to refer to a small-scale movement, apparently of borderline cases partly of Russian or Ukrainian blood. In general no rehabilitation has taken place. And this is in spite of the fact that settlers for the Crimea are still being called for even now.

Succeeding editions of the handbook *U.S.S.R.: Territorial Administrative Divisions of the Union Republics* carry appendices showing changes of place name. Thus the Chechen Urus-Martan is changed to Krasnoarmeiskoye in the 1954 edition, and this is reversed in the 1958 edition. Not all these changes are reversed, even in the Chechen case. For instance, the change of Novye Aldy to Chernorechiye remains.

But what is more striking is that each edition carries a whole new series of changes in the Crimea, invariably from Turkic to Russian — Lenino, Sovietski, Belogorsk and so on. What may be significant is the gradualness of the process. Though the population of the Crimea is now little less than it was in 1939, it seems to be much more concentrated in the coastal strip and the towns, and appeals for settlers imply that much of the old Tatar land is only gradually being repopulated. On this view the villages would be receiving Russian names as they were resettled by Russians.

Possible reasons for the special attitude to the Volga Germans and Crimean Tatars will be considered later.

L

Chapter 11

SHAMIL AGAIN

After Stalin's death the extremes of cultural Russification were modified a little. In 1954–6 the question of Tsarist conquest in general again became slightly controversial. And Shamil's case was at the centre of the controversy. At first it began to be cautiously maintained that Shamil's position could not be defined purely in terms of his being an 'Anglo-Turkish agent'. Then, at the end of 1955 and beginning of 1956, the question became bound up with a more general campaign against the old Stalinist falsifications which was conducted by the magazine *Questions of History* and its assistant editor Burdzhalov — encouraged by a sharp public attack by Mikoyan at the Twentieth Party Congress on certain Stalinist works of history. A stroke of luck for the rehabilitators was that it happened to have been Bagirov who had acted as Stalin's mouthpiece in attacking Shamil. He had fallen with Beria, and his execution was announced in April 1956. His statements could thus be freely attacked and no one could defend them.

A conference of readers of *Questions of History* held in Moscow, January 25th–28th, 1956, was the scene of a formal attempt to rehabilitate Shamil. A. M. Pikman spoke strongly for the pro-Shamil view, making the obvious enough point that those who shared his views 'for several years did not have the opportunity of stating their case in the press' (*Questions of History*, No. 2, 1956). Pikman, evidently with the support of Burdzhalov, followed this by an article forthrightly putting the case for Shamil and the Mountaineers (*Questions of History*, No. 3, 1956). Burdzhalov's campaign met with immediate resistance. A party

historian wrote revealingly (in *Questions of History*, No. 2, 1956)
that he deplored the re-evaluation of Shamil because 'it would
not further the strengthening of friendship among the nationalities' of the Soviet Union. But for the moment at least the
pro-Shamil historians had latitude to put their views forward.

Pikman's views were again strongly attacked in an article by
Bushuev (in *Questions of History*, No. 12, 1956), who even
asserted of the long and bitter Shamil wars that 'the incorporation of the Caucasus in Russia was of exceptional importance
. . . in the history of the (eventually) friendly Russo-Caucasian
relations'. But the same issue carried reports of two conferences
on the Shamil Question held at Makhachkala in Daghestan in
October and at the Academy of Sciences in Moscow in
November. At these the official line, put by N. A. Smirnov,
A. V. Fadeev and others, conceded the anti-colonial aspect of
the mountaineers' resistance, but stressed the reactionary
character of Muridism and the importance of Anglo-Turkish
imperialist support. A few speakers put forward an even more
strongly anti-Shamil view. But the great majority took a stand
favourable to the Imam and his followers on all counts.
Burdzhalov declared flatly, 'The Mountaineers were fighting
for their freedom and independence . . . what took place was
not unification but conquest'. I. Lavrov said it was a mistake
to 'approach history like politics projected into the past; we
need science which reveals the objective truth. In the struggle
of the Mountaineers the main thing is their struggle for freedom'. M. A. Mamakaev called the Turkish issue a red herring.
'The Mountaineers . . . wanted neither the knout of Nicholas I
nor the noose of the Janissaries: the Mountaineers were seeking
their own freedom and independence'. A. A. Abilov went to
the length of recalling that the Bolsheviks only obtained
Mountaineer support in the Revolution by appealing to the
Shamil tradition.

At about this time, too, the Bureau of the Daghestan
Communist Party repudiated a resolution it had made in
support of the Stalin-Bagirov view of Shamil in August 1950.
It issued orders for materials on Shamil to be restored to local

libraries and museums, and called for historical re-evaluation of events such as the rebellion of 1877.

The Shamil issue had in any case become entangled with the whole question of 'liberalization' in historiography. Burdzhalov had taken the decisions of the Twentieth Party Congress in February 1956 as permission to historians to seek out and publish the facts, to tell the truth as they saw it, and to maintain a variety of viewpoints. This was, as it soon appeared, a misinterpretation of the decrees of the Party leadership. Burdzhalov's own troubles were mainly due to his publishing unsuitable facts and inferences about the events of 1917 in Petrograd. The official counter-attack was an unsigned article 'Observe Strictly the Leninist Principle of "Partiinost" in Historical Science' which appeared in the dominating Party journal *Kommunist* (No. 4, 1957) (passed for the press in March 1957). This asserted that 'no one among serious Soviet scholars casts doubt on the progressive nature of the unification of the peoples of the Northern Caucasus with Russia'. It attacked Pikman and *Questions of History* as follows:

> The impression is generally formed that *Questions of History* sometimes uses the discussion section not in order to organize truly useful scientific discussions but to impose upon the readers its own biased viewpoint. A case in point is A. M. Pikman's article on Shamil's movement (No. 3, 1956), clamorous in tone, weak in argumentation, ignoring the level of scientific knowledge already attained.
>
> The author is 'diverted' from an analysis of the social structure of mountain society in the nineteenth century and from a class analysis of the movement itself . . . . A. Pikman justifies the religious-political system of the Imamat as allegedly being the inevitable and only possible form for an effective fight by the mountaineers against the Tsarist colonizers. In regard to the efforts by Britain and Turkey to use Shamil's movement for expansionist purposes, he is inclined to deny them altogether, seeing in this merely a perfectly justified effort by the mountaineers to seek support from anybody anywhere. He depicts Shamil as a champion of democracy, and tries to prove that it was only because of the weakness of the movement that Shamil 'was unable to establish a genuinely democratic administration'. The author of the article overlooks the fact that the movement led by

Shamil developed on a basis of semi-patriarchal, semi-feudal relationships, and that Muridism became the ideology of the militant feudal and clerical nobility. (*Kommunist*, No. 4, March 1957.)

At the same time it granted an 'anti-colonialist' element to Shamil's movement, and conceded that he was not an Anglo-Turkish agent pure and simple.

By the previous issue of *Questions of History*, its editorial board had lost seven of its previous members, including Burdzhalov. Smirnov, who had maintained an essentially anti-Shamil position, retained his post. Later issues of the periodical attacked Burdzhalov on various matters and Pikman for his Caucasian views.

In so far as the new attitude is slightly more liberal than that of Stalin's time it is welcome. But like the restoration of the deported nations it is an improvement suffering from one major difficulty. These concessions are quite simply made by fiat from the group of Russian rulers. The vicissitudes of Shamil's position show clearly enough that a line may be laid down and then amended, solely from above. Unless and until a complete change in the whole method of ruling the Soviet Union takes place, there is not the slightest guarantee that this will not be reversed, as the result of a change of mind in the Kremlin or, even more likely, as a result of some shift in the struggle for power among the leaders.

Moreover, relaxation of control over the subject nationalities in the Soviet Union must be expected in the long run to encourage centrifugal tendencies. But as soon as these are manifested, whoever rules in the Kremlin will be bound to try to tighten things up again. This is much what happened in Hungary in 1956. It may be argued that the nationalities would be well advised to accept what concessions are granted them, and not show any signs of wanting further extensions of national freedom. But this is not how national feeling works.

The 1956–7 controversy about Shamil seems to show various things. First, the majority of historians, and in particular those of the North Caucasus itself, favour an interpretation of the

Shamil movement in terms of its progressive national-liberation character, which also accords with proto-Marxist views. The Party leadership, on the other hand, seeks the imposition of a single 'scientific' estimate — which is to say, as with previous attitudes so described, one which is in accord with the political tactics of the moment. The extremes of repression and Russification which marked Stalin's last years are abandoned, by an extension natural in Soviet circumstances, as much in the case of the dead Shamil as of the living Chechens. The national hero is no longer to be smeared as a venal traitor. His movement's motives are admitted to be honourable. And in the present state of Soviet foreign policy in the Moslem world, Islam as such is not attacked directly. On the other hand there is no reversion to pre-Stalinist views about the essentially progressive nature of the mountaineers' struggle. With all the new concessions to local feeling, the essential is not conceded: nothing that justifies independence from Russia, in 1860 or 1958, is to be tolerated. Nor can Shamil's 'ideology', with its egalitarian-religious context, be treated with anything but hostility — though it must be as Muridist, rather than Islamic that it is condemned. On this last point Pikman had been particularly awkward, blurting out the unfortunate fact that

no special religious sect called Muridism existed at that period either in the Caucasus or in Turkey. One can talk about Islam as a religion but not about a special Muridist ideology. Under the guise of criticizing non-existent Muridism the general dogmas of Mohammedanism, allegedly many times worse than those of Christianity, are being criticized. (*Questions of History*, No. 12, 1956.)

It should be remarked that in their campaign in favour of the facts of history Burdzhalov and his colleagues carried the 'liberal' line much further than operators in any other field, except for some novelists and poets. The argument about Shamil was only one of many issues on which 1956 saw a struggle between the historians and the temporarily confused Department of Agitation and Propaganda of the Central Committee. *Questions of History* was much more sharply attacked for its attitude to party history, and in the winter of 1956–7 the heavy guns of not only *Kommunist*, but *Party Life* and *Pravda* itself, were brought to bear on the little fortress of objectivity, which was finally silenced.

For the Party the Shamil issue clearly represented the National Question pure and simple. And if the present solution (whereby both the Mountaineers and their conquerors were in a way fighting for progress, but the latter more so) is an illogical and shaky sort of compromise, the policy behind it is equally so. The present tendency seems to be to say as little as possible about the facts of Caucasian history, and to confine comment to very occasional repetition of the formula arrived at. The difficulties produced by the following up of the attack on Stalin by a very large measure of back-pedalling is even more acute in Party history. For instance, there has now been, for over two years, *no* official story at all, plausible or otherwise, about the rights and wrongs of the 1936–8 Trials. Any further historical rewriting awaits political developments, and this applies to Shamil too.

In general we may take the changes in the Soviet attitude to Shamil as illustrative of the whole progress of Communist nationality policy. In the earlier years of the regime everything was done to harness the whole immense prestige of the Imam to the service of the government: the national freedom he had fought for, it was alleged, had been attained by his Soviet successors. When it had become obvious that the nationalities had ceased to see the Soviet Union as answering their desire for independence, Shamil was denounced: as a symbol of resistance to Moscow rule, he was too exciting to the local population. Yet, as the post-Stalin regime seems to have felt, to forfeit this powerful symbolic figure to the enemy meant a dead loss, an admission that the nationalities could only be ruled by Russification and brute force. The present attitude can be seen as an attempt to make the best of the national traditions of the mountaineers, in so far as that is compatible with preserving the essence of the Stalinist position — that 'unification with Russia', in Shamil's time and now, is the overriding *summum bonum*.

Chapter 12

THE DEPORTEES RETURN

R eports now began to come in of the return of the deportees, and it soon became plain that their experiences in
the wilderness had not turned them into model Soviet
citizens, and that control had to be exerted by trustworthy
Russians.

Gorkin implied in his speech that the return of the smaller
of the nations in question was an easier matter than the repatriation of the Chechens. And in fact the smallest — the Balkars,
or some of them — began to arrive back almost immediately
after the law was published. *Sovietskaya Rossiya* of May 12th,
1957, reports a Balkar Kolkhoz on the Cherek celebrating the
return; and it announces, 'starting from April,' the publication
of a local newspaper *Kommunzinge Zhol* in Balkar. Smirnov's
History of Kabarda, passed for printing in May 1957, also asserts
that:

> The task of the economic rehabilitation of a significant number of
> Balkars was successfully carried out. The working people of the
> Republic showed all-sided help to the Balkars, and helped them
> to re-establish their kolkhozes and sovkhozes, public and private
> enterprises, and cultural and educational institutions. This
> brotherly help demonstrated the unbreakable comradeship of the
> peoples of the country.

Early in 1958 the British mountaineering expedition in the
Caucasus actually met a Balkar who praised the regime's
efforts.

The Karachai return does not seem to have been so quick.
Cherkessk Radio (April 8th, 1958) is reported as saying that

preparatory work had begun for the mass return of the Karachai. Stavropol Radio has been quoted as announcing the arrival of 5,000 Karachai families late in 1957 (*Caucasian Review*, No. 6, p. 151).

The reorganization of education had already been dealt with by the Ministry of Education of the R.S.F.S.R., which ruled that within four years Kalmyk, Karachai, Chechen and Ingush children should be taught in their native languages in Classes I–IV, and thereafter (V–X) in Russian, but that for the moment only the first class could be taught in the native language. This seems to confirm further that practically no native teachers were immediately available, and hence that normal education had not been practised in exile (*Narodnoe Obrazovanie*, May 1957).

The same article, in fact, called for the organizing of classes for the 'training or retraining of primary teachers', with the obvious implication that the deportees had been complete pariahs culturally as well as politically during their years in the wilderness. This is further confirmed by an article 'Brotherly collaboration of the Peoples of the U.S.S.R.' in the paper *Aid to Political Self-Education*, No. 10 (October 1957), which gives a list of scientific workers, in 1955, of all the main nationalities of the Soviet Union, including 70 Kabardines, 106 Yakuts, 90 Udmurts, 343 Ossetians, 231 Daghestan nationals, etc. (These figures are also printed in *Questions of Philosophy*, No. 5, 1957.) None of the purged nations are included. That the omission is not due to a mere desire not to mention these peoples is shown by the fact that the article goes on later to praise the Central Committee for re-establishing 'the national autonomy of the Balkar, Chechen, Ingush, Kalmyk and Karachai peoples' thus removing 'the infringements in the application of the Leninist principles of national policy which were committed during the war'.

We have already seen the meagre reports of the Kalmyk trickle home. But when it comes to the Chechens, it seems that the authorities were right to expect trouble of a different kind. At first reports gave no indication of anything but smooth progress. On June 21st, 1957, Moscow Radio announced that one Chechen and one Ingush paper were appearing in Grozny. Grozny Radio of October 29th, 1957, stated that 142,000 Chechens and Ingushi had 'so far settled in the autonomous republic'.

By the beginning of 1958 no regular government yet existed in the Chechen-Ingush Republic, which was ruled by an Organizing Committee. A crisis had meanwhile arisen. Instead of the 100,000 repatriates scheduled to have come back by then some 200,000 had returned and the committee was overwhelmed (*Groznenskii Rabochii*, January 12th, 1958). Homes and work for the repatriates and schools for their children were not available. Moreover, an article published in *Groznenskii Rabochii* (January 31st, 1958) revealed other problems. 'Reactionary elements', especially supporters of old custom and of the Shariya, were preserving tribal and religious survivals and discouraging the Chechens from playing an active part in social, political and labour life. There had been a revival of polygamy — one man being mentioned as having five wives. (This may, as Mr. Kolarz has suggested, reflect the extent of the number of Chechen males to have perished — just as in Paraguay, after the wars of the dictator Lopez almost exterminated the male population, polygamy had to be introduced.)

The article also speaks of national discord, and of Chechens and Ingushi who refused to let their children join Soviet Youth Clubs and other institutions for Communist indoctrination. It attacks the resettlers, too, for their opposition to work on the collective and state farms. 'Some backward elements put their private property first and show a criminal disregard for the social property of collective and state farms.' All Communists in the area are called upon to wage a ruthless struggle against survivals from the past in the minds of the Chechens and Ingushi. But the paper admits that even the officials chosen from the repatriates often support 'reactionary attitudes'. In addition 'backward elements' were trying 'to re-establish private property and plundering the property of the Kolkhozes and Sovkhozes'. This at least sounds as if Chechens and Ingushi are attempting to retrieve their own possessions, and that this is not well regarded by the authorities. The whole picture is one of peoples whose alienation from the Soviet system has been strengthened rather than weakened by their sufferings.

Pravda (March 19th, 1958) gives the names of those elected to the Soviet of the Union and the Soviet of Nationalities in the general election just held. Of the thirteen candidates elected to both houses from the Chechen-Ingush Republic six have Russian while the other seven have Muslim names. The First Secretary of the Republic is given as a Russian, Alexei Yakovlev, who had for years held the post of First Secretary of the old Grozny Province. The Second Secretary has a Chechen-sounding name. Another Russian elected is Secretary of one of the Raion committees (that of Sundzha). (That the republic still had no government other than the 'organizing committee' was indicated by the presence of the 'chairman' of that body, Gairbekov, evidently a Chechen.) A Women's Congress of the Chechen-Ingush A.S.S.R. on July 10th, 1957, had similarly had its main report from the Russian Novikova, 'Head of the Department of Science and Education' of the Party Provincial Committee. The other areas showed similar results. The First Secretary of the Kalmyk Autonomous Province was Nikolai Zhezhov.

One of the thirteen from the Chechen-Ingush Republic can be presumptively identified as an Ingush — since he comes from a State farm with the title 'Ingushi'. The location of this farm in the Malgobek area is an indication that that area has been allotted to the Ingushi. It is in the north-west corner of the Republic, in an area formerly Ingush.

Groznenskii Rabochii of March 25th, 1958, also referred to a plenary session of the Organizing Council, which had been concerned with improving political work among the Chechens and Ingushi. 'Political agitation is very poor among women and youth on collective farms and in rural areas in general.' Anti-religious propaganda was not operating properly, and 'too little attention was being given to the spirit of the Leninist nationalities policy'. A republican government was formed about this time, with Gairbekov as Chairman of the Council of Ministers (a title he is given on Moscow Radio of April 16th, 1958).

A 'meeting recently held of the provincial party *Aktiv* of the Chechen-Ingush Republic' was reported in *Pravda* of September 2nd, 1958. N. G. Ignatov, member of the Presidium of the Central Committee, and of the Party Secretariat, took part — an extraordinarily high official to be present on such an occasion. 'Sharp criticism' was made of the Provincial Committee and the Grozny town committee, which had committed 'serious shortcomings' in industry, agriculture and ideological work, and the 'isolation of many Party and Soviet organs from the masses' was deplored. 'Sharp criticism' was also levelled against the provincial secretaries — Yakovlev, Saiko, Cherkevich, Fornenko and Sagaev, and against the Chairman of the Council of Ministers Gairbekov. (At least three of the secretaries' names are Slavonic.)

In all these reports the impression is given that the guarantee not to harm established economic interests is being interpreted to mean that the Chechens, in the main, are having to fit in as best they can into Russian Kolkhozes, and to provide a reserve of labour for the industries of Grozny. Right from the start, for instance, there have been accounts for the building of new houses for them: *Grozny Radio* of October 29th, 1957, spoke of 9,000 new ones with 11,500 under construction; *Groznenskii Rabochii* of January 12th, 1958, mentioned 15,000 built in rural areas also, and 'thousands' under construction. There is no need to assume that this is an overestimate — the houses of the area are simple, hut-like constructions. But it does seem to imply that the Chechens and Ingushi are not getting their own homes and villages back, but are rather being directed where the state desires — including the hitherto non-Chechen desert area to the north of the Terek which for the first time forms part of the republic and is shown as Chechen on ethnographical maps.

The other point that emerges clearly enough is that the Chechens are unco-operative, addicted to ideological, social and economic practices disliked by the regime, and in general still possessed by a desire not to be under their present rulers.

How Many Came Back?

Some reasons have already been given for thinking that the Kalmyks and Karachai are considerably reduced in numbers. The *Encyclopaedia* (second edition, Vol. 40, 1958) now gives the population of the Stavropol territory as Russian, and 'also Ukrainian, Cherkess, Karachai, Kalmyk, Nogay, Abazin, Armenian, Ossetian, Turkmen, etc.' It looks as if the order of naming may be the order of the size of the population figures. The Nogay component is small (there were 10,000 in the whole North Caucasus in 1926, according to the first edition of the *Encyclopaedia*, Vol. 42), and the last four, too, only amount to a few thousands. The conclusion seems to be that the Karachai and Kalmyks (or at the least those who had returned by the end of November 1957) are now smaller in numbers than the Cherkess (this term would include the Adygei of the Adygei Autonomous Province, and give a total of 88,000, in 1939); and also that the Karachai are now more numerous than the Kalmyks — in this case without a time qualification, as there is no reason to expect that the Karachai return was to be, or was, quicker than that of the Kalmyks. All this is speculative, but it fits with the other information.

In the same way the article on the Karachai-Cherkess Autonomous Province in Volume 51 of the *Encyclopaedia* (second edition, 1958) says that the basic population is 'Cherkess and Karachai' in that order. And the article on Kalmykia in the same volume speaks of the 'greatest part of the population' being 'Russian and Kalmyk' in that order. It is significant that in the article on the Chechen-Ingush A.S.S.R. the Russians are listed second, after the Chechen-Ingushi. Since this is at a time when the A.S.S.R.s population is given as 700,000, and the return of only 200,000 Chechen-Ingushi had been announced, it is clear either that it is intended to refer (as an *Encyclopaedia* might be expected to) to the final results, or that the presence of any significant number of autochthones is sufficient to get them listed first. Either assumption would imply the existence of comparatively few Kalmyks. (And in the case of the Karachai-Cherkess A.P. Russians are not mentioned at all, though they must have numbered more than half the population, 214,000, in 1956. The Cherkess, 65,000 in 1939, could not have doubled in the intervening period, and there is no reason to believe that many of them have left the area.)

At the time of writing, the statistical evidence about the total numbers of survivors returning to the republics is rather indirect. We have seen some reasons for supposing that the Kalmyks, and perhaps the Karachai, have been seriously reduced in numbers.

Some population figures have become available in 1958, though they are a little difficult to assess. Volume 51 of the *Encyclopaedia* gives the following populations for the newly restored republic and provinces.

Chechen-Ingush A.S.S.R.	- -	*c.* 700,000 (1958)
Kalmyk A.S.S.R. -	- -	163,500 (1958)
Karachai-Cherkess A.P.	-	214,000 (1956)

There are articles also on each of the five rehabilitated *peoples*, but in each case the 1939 numbers are given, with a note that that is the date of the figure.

Earlier in the year the official handbook *U.S.S.R.: Administrative Territorial Divisions of the Union Republics* (Moscow, 1958) gave the populations as follows, as of April 1956:

Chechen-Ingush A.S.S.R.	- -	544,000
Kalmyk A.S.S.R. -	- -	118,000
Karachai-Cherkess A.P.	-	214,000

The Karachai-Cherkess figure is thus identical with the 1956 figures in the *Encyclopaedia*, while the Chechen one is identical with one described as 'April 1956 estimate' in Volume 47 of that publication. If it is true that, as said in *Groznenskii Rabochii* of January 12th, 1958, 200,000 Chechens and Ingushi had returned to their republic by early 1958, it would mean that at least 44,000 (or 8 per cent) of the Russians had left in the same period, assuming that the estimates have not, for some reason, been adjusted downwards meanwhile, nor one given of a date earlier than the estimate of 200,000 repatriates.

If, as a very rough guide, we tentatively apply this to the Kalmyk figures, subtracting 8 per cent of 118,000 to indicate a proportional Russian exodus — i.e. *c.* 9,400, and then taking the difference between the figures for the two years, we get a Kalmyk total of about 59,000. There are a number of unprovable assumptions involved. In the first place there may have been no Russian withdrawal from Kalmykia, even if there was one from Chechnia, and the Kalmyks may merely have filled the empty rural districts: on this assumption there would be only 48,000 of them.

The more likely interpretation is perhaps that the figures for 1958 are based on estimates made before the Grozny announcement about the return of the 200,000 Chechen-Ingushi. Grozny Radio of October 29th, 1957, announced that 'so far 142,000 members of these national groups have settled in the autonomous republic', so that an estimate made at that moment, adding the Russian population of 1956 to the returned Chechen-Ingushi, would have been 686,000. A week or two later and it could have been the round 700,000, which, in any case, is given as approximate. Exact registration of the return must be very difficult, and it does not seem unreasonable to imagine an estimate made for the first days of 1958, and soon proving inaccurate owing to the unexpected and unwelcome extra rush of Chechens. In this case the Kalmyk figure for early 1958 would be 45,500, with little indication that many more were expected. Unless heavily recruited from near-Kalmyk nations like the Oirots, it seems fairly plain at least, that the Kalmyks now number not more than some 90,000-110,000, making the most favourable assumptions, and may well be considerably fewer.

We can approach the matter from the other tack. In the same work the Karachai-Cherkess Autonomous Province's 1956 total of 214,000 compares with the 1941 figures for the former separated Karachai and Cherkess Autonomous Provinces of over 242,000, in 1941. This indicates an influx of non-Karachai of

214,000 minus the difference between the pre-war population (242,000) and the number of Karachai deportees (76,000), i.e. 66,000, which is the first reasonably definite indication of the extent of Russian settlement. If we assume (as seems certain) that the *Administrative-Territorial Divisions* figures are pre-rehabilitation, we get about 344,000 *new* non-autochthonous settlers in Checheno-Ingushetia, and about 60,000 in Kalmykia.

In any case, the reduced figures for 1956 as compared with 1939 show certainly that though a non-autochthonous influx has taken place, it has not been sufficient to repopulate the areas completely. If the 1958 figures are final, or nearly so, they indicate that the survivors *plus* most of the new Russian settlers form total populations either only just as large, or actually smaller, than the total present in 1939.

In the ethnographical section of Volume 50 of the *Encyclopaedia* (August 1957), figures are given for the speakers of various languages. In most of the tables of population it is stated that the figures derive from the pre-war census, and though nothing is said about dates in this case, the assumption would be that it was so here too — particularly as the later Volume 51 is careful to use only 1939 figures for *all* the deported peoples. But there is one anomaly. The figures given are:

> Chechen-Ingush speakers — about 500,000
> Kalmyk — about 130,000
> Balkar-Karachai — 87,000.

The first two are identical with the pre-war figures, but the last is much smaller — showing a decrease of no less than 31,000 — over 25 per cent. This, if spread evenly, would imply a reduction of the Balkars from *c.* 43,000 to *c.* 30,000 and of the Karachai from *c.* 76,000 to *c.* 57,000. (In fact the Karachai are likely to have suffered rather more severely than their neighbours.)

To assume that all three figures are post-war means to allow for an odd coincidence in the case of the Chechen-Ingushi and the Kalmyks and to assume that, for some reason, population-reducing factors which hit the Karachai-Balkars heavily had no effect on the others. This is, obviously, most unlikely. And even if the Chechens are now as numerous as in 1939, which seems not quite beyond the bounds of possibility, many considerations imply that the Kalmyks are not. The probability, therefore, is that these figures are pre-war in the case of the first two groups and new in the Karachai-Balkar case. This is odd, but not impossible: for instance some sort of pilot census might have been taken with the smaller group involved. But we cannot quite exclude the possibility that earlier considerations are misleading and that the Kalmyks have survived better than the Karachai-Balkars; or, that they have been recruited from fellow-nationals among their equally nomadic co-religionists on the borders of Soviet Asia.

On the other hand, the failure of Volume 51, appearing later, to give any recent estimates — sticking, as it does, to the 1939 Census — may signify that later and presumably more accurate counts proved disappointing.

On the Chechens and Ingushi even the announced return by January 1958 of 200,000, shows that the nation still exists in good numbers, though the final total is not implied. It would be interesting, also, to know the comparative number of men, women and children respectively: a polygamous nation (even if, as in this case, illegally so) can build up its numbers again very rapidly, even after very great losses among adult males.

A comparison of the 1941 and 1958 editions of *U.S.S.R.: Administrative Territorial Divisions of the Union Republics* shows that of the 697,408 living in the Chechen-Ingush A.S.S.R. at the time of the 1939 census, 498,739 lived in villages and 198,669 in towns (Grozny 172,500), while the 1956 estimate was 273,000 in villages, 271,000 in towns (Grozny 226,000). Moreover the size, at least, of the rural area had increased in the new frontiers. Very few of the town population used to be Chechen before the deportation — less than 10 per cent in 1936. Even in 1943, it was stated (*Large Soviet Encyclopaedia*, Vol. 51) as a claim that there were 5,000 Chechen workers in Grozny. In any case the rural deficit of 226,000 might have

M

been expected to mean that the 1957 influx of 200,000 Chechens could be absorbed without much trouble. The implication might be that the authorities' objection was more that they could not be smoothly fitted into the official view of what they should do and where. There had not been overpowering administrative difficulties about fitting them into Kazakh and Kirghiz areas all at once, and at a few weeks' notice, in 1944.

What proportion of the total survivors is represented by the 200,000 Chechens and Ingushi who had returned by 1958, is uncertain. On the one hand, the considerable extension of the new republic, not paralleled by the other rehabilitated units might imply that a population larger than that of 1939, (already reached) is to be absorbed. Admittedly the new area is desert and semi-desert steppe, hitherto inhabited only by a few thousand Tatar herdsmen; but part of the Chechen deportees have been living in only slightly better areas in Kazakhstan, and might be expected to cope. But much of the area can scarcely be intended to absorb more than a few tens of thousands, at least for many years.

And, on the other hand, there are a few signs that not many Chechens are left in Kazakhstan. Volume 50 of the second edition *Large Soviet Encyclopaedia*, the composite volume on the U.S.S.R., has a long article on the Kazakh S.S.R. Its population is still given as 'Kazakh, Russian, Ukrainian, Uzbek, Uigur, Dungan, etc.', with no Chechens. It is true that there have been announcements of Chechens cultural activities there till quite recently, but these are sometimes, of course, practised by very small minorities indeed, and in any case there was a reference in Gorkin's speech to Chechens who may choose to remain in Central Asia. References to the abolition of various village Soviets in Kazakhstan (e.g. *Kazakhstanskaya Pravda*, August 2nd, 1958) may perhaps refer in some cases to points depopulated by the emigration of Chechens and others.

It may be noted that even with the deportation of the Crimean Tatars the population of the Crimea is now given (in

Administrative Territorial Divisions) as 1,119,000, only a few thousand fewer than the 1,126,824 given for 1939. But A.S.S.R.s in which deportation did not take place all show increases in population. The handbook also gives another rather indirect indication of depopulation. That is, the decline in the number of village Soviets:

In the Chechen-Ingush A.S.S.R. -	225 in 1941;	154 in 1958
In Kalmykia - - - -	121 ,, ,, ;	52 ,, ,,
In the Kabardine-Balkar A.S.S.R.	116 ,, ,, ;	89 ,, ,,
In the Karachai-Cherkess A.P. -	97 ,, ,, ;	44 ,, ,,
	(53 of them Karachai)	

It is of course true that several factors operate to reduce the number of villages, or at least of village Soviets, all over the U.S.S.R. The flow of population to the towns has been accompanied by a considerable amount of fusion of collective farms into larger units. Yet there are other factors to be taken into account. In the first place scattered mountain villages are less easy to unite, even administratively, than those on the great plains. And the same applies, to some extent, to the widely scattered Kalmyk settlements.

The official *U.S.S.R. Economy: A Statistical Abstract* (English edition, Lawrence and Wishart, 1958) gives the decrease in the number of village Soviets throughout the Union as from 70,034 in 1941 to 50,516 in 1956 and in a footnote attributes the shrinkage to the amalgamation of collective farms which commenced in 1950.

The Kabardine-Balkar figures actually show *less* decrease than those of the U.S.S.R. as a whole, which may confirm this view of mountain peculiarity. The Chechen-Ingush figures are little below average. And those of the Karachai-Cherkess A.P. and the Kalmyk A.P. show a very much greater shrinkage. On the whole this seems to give some slight extra strength to the view that the Kalmyk villages in particular were not much occupied by Russians, and that therefore little exodus of Russians is now to be expected from Kalmykia even if it does take place from Checheno-Ingushetia, which is doubtful.

A further slight peculiarity was that the Moscow press of January 5th, 1958, printed a full list of the constituencies for the elections to the Supreme Soviet scheduled for March 16th, in which the rehabilitees voted. In principle the Soviet constituency represents a population of 300,000. And though there are a number where the population is really rather smaller, the same sort of effort is made in the U.S.S.R. as in the West to reshuffle electoral boundaries to fit population changes, from election to election. Both the 1950 and the 1954 elections showed the emergence of a number of new constituencies in areas where the population is known to have increased — that is mainly in the districts of continuing Russian colonization in Siberia and Central Asia. The 1958 list shows a number of changes as compared to that of 1954. For instance, six new constituencies have emerged in Kazakhstan, representing in theory at least an influx of 1,800,000 people, presumably mainly in connection with the Virgin Lands scheme. So it is interesting to compare the position in the North Caucasus. Here there has been very little change. In particular resettlement of the Chechens and Ingushi has not yet led to the creation of additional constituencies.

One trouble with this attempt to analyse the figures at present available is, leaving aside the difficulties of determining quite what they mean and when, that they may be quite wrong. Even with sedentary, well-registered populations estimates have proved surprisingly unsound. For instance in an interview on Radio Moscow on May 8th, 1958, P. G. Podyachev, Deputy Head of the U.S.S.R. Statistical Board and Director of the All-Union Population Census, said that a test census taken in the town of Stalino on August 1st, 1957, had shown the actual population to be about 642,000, whereas the town Executive Committee believed it (at the beginning of 1956) to be 828,000 while a calculation of the statistical board had given it as 625,000. Thus the figures in use in the U.S.S.R. seem to be significantly and in some cases wildly inaccurate.

A census covering the whole Union took place from 15th and 22nd January, 1959, and should give some important information, though no doubt it will be some time before the analysis and publication of the results. The questions include the nationality and the mother-tongue of members of the population. There has not been a census since 1939, and the results of that one are in some respects dubious. Its object was to replace the suppressed results, never yet published, of one taken in 1938. Facts and figures then emerging seem to have been unpalatable to the authorities, and the census officials were liquidated for sabotage. The objections, of which the main one seems to have been that the death-rate was shown as exceedingly high, are said to have included the unsatisfactory nature of the answers to the nationality question. Many members of minorities put themselves down as Russians, in order to improve their position vis-à-vis the authorities, and this is believed to have given unsuitably large Russian populations in the minority republics.

But the census will certainly provide more accurate, or at least more exact, figures than are available at the time of writing. So many motives exist for statistical inflation in that operation, however, that even when its results are published the points advanced in this chapter may be a useful check. In fairness it should be said that though, in principle, political misrepresentation of statistics might reasonably be expected from those who plainly distort other forms of fact, such as those of history, yet lately (in the period 1953–8 at least) there does not seem to have been any falsification of clear-cut absolute figures. In 1953, for instance, the Soviet Government condemned, and apparently abandoned, the previous practice of representing as the crop yield not what was actually collected, but an estimate of what ought to have been. This is not to say that, if a new Stalinist period is upon us, as is sometimes feared, direct falsification will not return. But meanwhile manipulation of genuine statistics for propaganda purposes is the normal method, and this would not affect the original absolute figures, if made available.

On the other hand there are certain improvements which could be achieved without falsification. In particular, the case of the Kalmyks has evidently been given much thought by the Soviet government, almost certainly because of the effect in Buddhist Asia. It would be particularly easy to supplement the Kalmyks by inducing a few tens of thousands of immigrants of their own stock, language, religion and habits of life to join them in the steppe — Oirots, Buryats or Mongols.

Preliminary results were given in *Pravda* of May 10th, 1959. These did not include a breakdown by nations, but did give the populations by area. The relevant figures were:

Chechen-Ingush A.S.S.R.	- -	711,000
Kalmyk A.S.S.R. - -	- -	183,000
Karachai-Cherkess A.P.	- -	277,000

Using the same methods, it will readily be seen that this gives *minimum* numbers as follows:

Chechens and Ingushi	- - -	167,000
Kalmyks - - -	- -	65,000
Karachai - - -	- -	63,000

(or rather less if we make allowance for the natural increase in the Russian population since 1956). On the other hand, these are hard figures and previous ones are estimates. And we do not know how many Russians, if any, have left the areas.

By the time of the 1959 census *all* the Kalmyks and Karachai should have returned, but the Chechens and Ingushi were expected not to complete their resettlement until 1960, and it is impossible to be certain about them, let alone about how accurate the 200,000 estimate made the previous year may have been. If we stick to the Kalmyks and Karachai we certainly form an impression of greater loss than some of the intermediate estimates imply. Even if there has been *no increase whatever* in the Russian population of Kalmykia as between the 1939 and the 1959 figures, the number of Kalmyks must have decreased in that period by *c.* 38,000—to *c.* 96,000. In practice the assumption is obviously most conservative, and it would be surprising if as many as 75,000 survive.

Meanwhile we can only say that there are some statistical as well as other reasons to believe that the Kalmyks have been reduced to not more than a few score thousands, and the Karachai considerably, though not quite so catastrophically, while the Chechen-Ingushi may perhaps number three-fifths, or more, of their original strength — if we could assume that the schedule of 100,000 returning in 1957 had been intended to apply equally to all the four years of reconstruction they would even have recovered to the level of 400,000, four-fifths of their pre-war numbers. In the period 1926 to 1939 they increased by about 27 per cent in spite of risings, collectivization and general trouble, and they might have shown again, in Kazakhstan, a demographic resilience as striking as the apparently unquenchable national spirit they are continuing to show in their newly regained homes.

Summary of Estimates by Various Methods

1. Assuming the figures of language speakers in Vol. 50 of the *Encyclopaedia* are *all* contemporary, correct and final:

Chechens and Ingushi	-	*c.* 500,000
Kalmyks - - - -		130,000
Karachai and Balkars	-	87,000 ? Karachai 57,000
		? Balkars 30,000

2. (*a*) Assuming the order of naming (*b*) ditto *in the Stavro-*
   in the republics represents the   *pol Territory*
   relative populations and is
   final (with no new Russian
   emigration allowed for):

Chechens and Ingushi	-	>350,000	
Kalmyks - - - -		<80,000	*c.* 70,000
Karachai - - - -		*c.* 75,000	*c.* 75,000

3. Assuming that those planned to return per annum represent a regular flow over the years of reinstatement, and that the plan has not been exceeded where no complaint has been made:

Chechens and Ingushi	-	400,000
Kalmyks - - - -		90,000
Karachai - - - -		?
Balkars - - - -		?

4. Minimum fairly reliably deduced actually to exist:

Chechens and Ingushi	-	-	-		200,000
Kalmyks	-	-	-	-	65,000
Karachai	-	-	-	-	63,000
Balkars	-	-	-	-	?

It will be seen that rigour is unattainable, and that these estimates depend on assumptions that can be varied.

A very rough estimate, with 'about' standing for a possible error of at least 25 per cent each way, might be:

Chechens	-	-	-	c.	275,000
Ingushi	-	-	-	c.	50,000
Kalmyks	-	-	-	c.	70,000
Karachai	-	-	-	c.	65,000
Balkars	-	-	-	c.	30,000
					490,000

A minimum estimate, in so far as one can be based on official figures, might be about 350,000.

The maximum estimate (under method 1) gives 717,000. This is less than the 752,000 of the 1939 numbers of these nations, while other Soviet nationalities have increased. Nor will any present-day figure show the losses of the 1943–5 period. Not only are these masked by thirteen years of births, but premature death struck disproportionately at the old people and the young children, neither of them categories actively affecting the birth-rate over the intervening years. In the cases where death was due to resistance rather than to conditions, adult males would have suffered most. But in races having anyhow no theoretical objection to polygamy, this too might be expected not to affect the birth-rate critically. It is true that the conditions of life cannot have been favourable to infant survival, but it is common experience that great population increases take place in conditions of extreme poverty and with an accompaniment of high infant-mortality.

Meanwhile the Crimean Tatars and Volga Germans, representing about 43 per cent of the deportees, remain in exile.

The 1959 census figures were given in *Pravda* on February 4, 1960, as follows:

	Thousands	*Percentage regarding the language in question as their native tongue*	
Chechens	418	98·8	i.e. 413,000
Ingushi	106	97·9	i.e. 104,000
Kalmyks	106	91·0	i.e. 96,000
Karachai	81	73·9	i.e. 60,000
Balkars	42	97·0	i.e. 41,000

The ways in which these figures, allowing for two years of natural increase, confirm or conflict with earlier official statements, and conclusions based on them by the author, will be apparent. The language-nationality differentiation is particularly interesting: (in the case of the 1,619,000 Germans noted, only 75 per cent are given as using their own tongue).

Chapter 13

SOVIET VIEWS

————⟨◦⟩⟨◦⟩⟨◦⟩————

W e have already traced the Soviet attitude to the victimized peoples in the successive editions of the *Large Soviet Encyclopaedia*. Two more stages remain which can be followed in that authoritative compilation. First there is the set of regular volumes coming out after *SIG* in 1956, and in particular after the public decrees in February 1957. In these the new administrative frontiers are given on the map, the existence of the nations and their republics and provinces is referred to, but next to nothing is actually said about them. It is not until the publication in mid-1958 of a supplementary volume (51), already promised in Volume 50, that positive statements and full-scale articles appear, a line having presumably been debated and settled on, for the time being at least.

The only deported people who had not been in the part of the alphabet covered in the volumes of the *Encyclopaedia* which came out during the period of silence were the Chechens. But when Volume 47, which could have contained the Chechen information was reached in April 1957, it contained only a few lines on the *Chechen-Ingush A.S.S.R.* The entire article was as follows:

> Forming part of the R.S.F.S.R., situated in the North Caucasus. Its area is 19·3 sq. kilometres and its population 544,000 (April 1956 estimate). It is divided into 16 regions, has 3 cities and 3 settlements of city type. Further see: Volume 51 Chechen-Ingush A.S.S.R.

Thus the existence of the Republic, though not yet of its peoples, was acknowledged, but all comment postponed.

The last of the regular volumes of the *Large Soviet Encyclopaedia* to come out were the new composite volume on the U.S.S.R., Volume 50, passed on August 15th, 1957, and Volume 40, passed on November 20th, 1957. This last was delayed for about eighteen months, the reason without any doubt being that it contained the article on Stalin, now five pages as against the forty-six in the first edition. It also has articles on the Stavropol Territory and the Stalingrad Province. By this time the Stalingrad Province, into which part of the Kalmyk A.S.S.R. had been incorporated, had lost that area and this is shown on the map.

The full territorial reorganizations due to the re-establishment of the Chechen-Ingush and the Kabardine-Balkar republics and the setting up of the Karachai-Cherkess and Kalmyk autonomous provinces are shown for the first time on the map of the Stavropol Territory, which now included the two autonomous provinces mentioned and bordered on the two republics. (They are seen too, though less clearly, in the ethnographical and administrative maps in Volume 50.) The description of the Stavropol Territory states 'into the composition of the Territory enter the *Karachai-Cherkess Autonomous Province* (q.v.) and the Kalmyk Autonomous Province'. The first of these provinces is put in italics but the second not, any more than it is followed by a q.v. Any attempt to look up the Karachai-Cherkess Autonomous Province would have been fruitless until the appearance of the supplementary Volume 51. Yet that has a Kalmyk article too and if the reference is to Volume 51, one wonders why it cannot apply in both cases. Possibly the 'Karachai-Cherkess (q.v.)' is intended to refer the reader to the article on the Cherkess Autonomous Province, in Volume 47. This is a brief note (see p. 136). The period of deportations and disloyalties in the area is referred to only in the form that 'from August 1942 to January 1943 the territory of the Stavropol Territory was occupied by the German Fascist robbers' and this is said to have caused economic losses.

The administrative maps referred to show the Kalmyk

Autonomous Province as almost exactly on the area of the old
Kalmyk Republic. Some of the Russified names have been
changed back into Kalmyk — in particular Elista, the capital.
Others remain in their Russified form. The Karachai area, now
united with the Cherkess Autonomous Province, also seems to
occupy almost exactly its old territory. The Kabardine-Balkar
Republic is shown. It has regained from Georgia the Balkar
strip round Mount Elbruz.

Autonomous Republics and Provinces in the North Caucasus 1958

A more interesting state of affairs is shown in the frontiers
further east. The Chechen-Ingush Republic is not in the same
frontiers. Some Ingush territory taken by Ossetia has not been
regained. Instead the Chechen-Ingush A.S.S.R. has been
compensated by a much larger stretch to the north of the
Terek, in land of which large areas are shown on the accompanying map as 'sand'. A further reorganization has taken
place here. The whole of the sparsely inhabited desert and semi-
desert stretch between the Terek and the Kuma formed part of

Daghestan up till the beginning of the war when it was annexed to Russia proper. It has now been restored to Daghestan, except for the part given to the Chechen-Ingushi.

Some light on the resettlement of the mountaineers in the plains is thrown by the article by A. Agayev in *Literature and Life* of May 1959. It speaks of 'the problem of resettling the hillman in the plains, a problem which is so burning for Daghestan that the C.C. C.P.S.U. dealt with it at its Plenary Meeting in December 1958. This resettlement would guarantee to all socially gainful employment. It promises a well-to-do life and lighter working conditions. It makes it possible to discard the wooden plough for the tractor and the cart for the lorry. It means roads instead of mountain paths, and good dwellings. At the present moment the Republic's Party organisation is carrying on a tireless effort to explain the idea to the hillmen, persuading them to resettle in the plains which take up nearly half of this 'land of mountains'. But many of the hillmen, while they understand that life in the plains is a blessing, are not hastening to resettle there. In the past the plains meant foreign incursions, hostility on the part of the local population, malaria and droughts. Force of habit is also a great obstacle'.

In fact they do not want to go, and the same presumably applies to the Chechens.

The ethnographical maps in Volume 50 are equally interesting. The Kalmyk, Karachai and Chechen-Ingush territories are now shown striped alternately with the colours of the local peoples and those of the Russians — though Balkaria is given as solid Balkar. The Ingushi are shown, as far as can be distinguished from the extremely small-scale map in question, as a very small corner of one of the Chechen stripes.

The Crimea is given striped Russian and Ukrainian simply. No Tatars are shown there. (But two small Jewish areas are designated.)

No Germans are given anywhere on the territory of the U.S.S.R., though minorities as small as the Gypsies are indicated.

Unlike the first volume no definite new table of nationalities and numbers is given. But in the ethnographical section the figures already looked at in Chapter 12 are given for the speakers of the various languages.

The Tatars are not divided by numbers into their separate groups though a simple list of these groups is given which does not mention the Crimean Tatars. And the only reference to Germanic languages is as follows: 'To the Germanic languages belongs Yiddish, the language of a certain part of the Jewish population of the U.S.S.R.'

Volume 51 was passed for publication in April 1958. It rehabilitated a number of unpersons, and the restored un-nations too. In the case of none of the executed individuals did it say how they met their deaths. And the lowest minimum was said about the equivalent event in the lives of the deported races. In the case of the personalities, several curious points came to light. Two of these, as affecting the accuracy of Soviet statements, are relevant to this enquiry. Mamia-Ivan Orelak-hashvili, the Georgian Party leader, has an article, which says he died in 1940. *Pravda* of December 20th, 1937, had announced that he had been sentenced to death and that 'the sentence has been carried out'. Krylenko, another prominent Communist to fall in the purges is given as dying in 1938. In *Memoirs of Lenin* published only in 1956, his date of death is given as 1940.

The work of the editors of the second edition of the *Encyclopaedia* is summed up in Volume 51 in which is printed all relevant matter. The editors mention that 15,820 writers contributed, and give their nationalities. Thirty-six Soviet nations are listed, down to small ones like the Cherkess and the Lesghians, but none of the deported races.

In none of the articles on the peoples and their areas is a figure for national numbers given that is later than 1939. There are articles on the Balkars ($\frac{1}{2}$ column), Ingushi ($\frac{3}{4}$ column), Ingush Language ($\frac{1}{2}$ column), Kalmyks ($\frac{1}{2}$ column), Karachai ($\frac{1}{3}$ column), Chechen, Chechen Language and Chechen-Ingush A.S.S.R. (11 pages for the three), the Karachai-Cherkess A.P.

(4½ pages), and the Kalmyk A.P. (nearly 3 pages). In addition an extra loose page has been slipped in pointing out that the Kalmyk A.P. later became an A.S.S.R., and providing a map of it.

In general it may be said that these articles return, though only up to a point, to the views of the pre-deportation first edition, thus bringing these people's official history in line once more with that of other Soviet minorities.

The Chechen-Ingush A.S.S.R. article, which may again be taken as typical, starts with a long summary of what appears to be admirable research work done since the first edition (which said that 'almost nothing is known' of the peoples' history before the seventeenth century) into earlier times. Identifications are made with tribes mentioned by Strabo and Armenian writers, and it is concluded on these and archaeological grounds that the Chechen-Ingushi are 'aborigines of the North Caucasus'.

The gradual conversion to Islam, starting in the seventeenth century, the first clash with Russia in 1732, the rise of Urshuma are detailed. Then come the Murids. 'The movement of the mountaineers, clothed in the religious cloak of reactionary Muridism, had deep social and economic reasons'. Shamil, 'by cruel methods succeeded in breaking the resistance of the feudalists of Daghestan . . . and united tens of varilingual tribes of mountaineers into one state unity.' He was defeated because the Tsar was stronger, but also because

> in Shamil's movement itself were lodged insoluble internal contradictions. While annihilating the Avar Khans, and professing the equality of all Muslims before the Shariya, Shamil in the long run created a new feudalizing autocracy in the persons of the naibs and other officials, which oppressed the people no less than the Russian generals and officials.

This resulted in a popular movement for peace with Russia. Tsarist oppression is described in strong terms, but 'at the same time, the unification of Chechnia and Russia promoted the economic and social development of the Chechen-Ingush people'.

In the Revolution Soviet power was established in Chechnia 'amid great difficulties, fierce class war, bloody battles'. Afterwards struggles against the kulaks, who used religious and national propaganda, and 'a stubborn struggle to liquidate' the Sharia, are described. And we are back with the remarks about national satisfaction which appeared in the first edition. They read even more peculiarly in retrospect, after the deportation, than in prospect. For instance it might seem, in the circumstances, to require a little nerve to write: 'Soviet power freed the toiling masses of Checheno-Ingushetia from national oppression and liquidated national inequality.'

The historical section of the article consists of approximately two and a half pages from earliest times up to the Revolution, one page from the Revolution till 1920, half a page from 1920 to 1939 and a quarter of a column from 1939 to 1957. The events of the war are given as that 'the toilers of the Chechen-Ingush A.S.S.R. reconstructed their economy and actively assisted the front', that the Germans reached the area but were defeated, and that in 1944 5,000 Chechen and Ingush workers were in jobs in oil and other undertakings in Grozny.

Later happenings are presented as follows:

In 1944 the Chechen-Ingush A.S.S.R. was liquidated. In accordance with a decree of the Presidium of the Supreme Soviet of the U.S.S.R. of January 9th, 1957, the Chechen-Ingush A.S.S.R. was re-established.

There is also a cultural portion which mentions the appearance in 1956, in Kazakhstan and Kirghizia, of two collections of Chechen literature, and says that in 1957 a conference of Chechen-Ingush writers was called, to 'define new tasks before the national literature'.

The other articles are similar. That on the Karachai-Cherkess A.P. mentions as one of the characteristics of Tsarist colonialism that 'Russian officials sat in the administrative apparatus and the courts'. It does not refer to the liquidation of the Karachai A.P. at all, giving simply the administrative change of January 9th, 1957.

That on the Kalmyk A.P. describes the Tsarist oppressions

of the nineteenth century very clearly. After the Revolution 'bandit detachments recruited by feudal, kulak and nationalist elements' were liquidated, and then the kulaks, who 'offered bitter resistance'. The liquidation of the Kalmyk republic itself is mentioned in the same terms as in the Chechen-Ingush article. The culture section reveals that a paper in Russian and Kalmyk (*Halumg Unn — Sovietskaya Kalmykia*) is coming out in Elista. A collection *Light on the Steppes* has been published, and in general 'the national and social renaissance of the Kalmyk people began after the victory of the great October Socialist Revolution'.

The articles on the peoples as such are brief and mainly about economy and folk crafts and arts. But it is also claimed that 'in Soviet times Balkar literature was created' and so on, and that the nations were backward until Soviet times. The religious affiliation of 'the believing section' of the nation is often given. And there is one revealing point on the Kalmyks: 'with the unification in kolkhozes, they became settled.'

The comparisons with the previous edition hardly need labouring. In general one may say that the present line is:

(a) to describe their resistance to Tsarism as well intentioned up to a point, but leading only to local despotism, to which 'unification' with Russia was preferable, on account of its progressive effects.
(b) to say little or nothing about recent unpleasantnesses.
(c) to claim the nations as grateful, and rightly grateful, to the Soviet system.

There is one other article relevant to the deportations. General Serov, who was not thought important enough for one in 1955, in the regular volume, has now been given space. Of his services in the war it is said that he 'carried out assignments of the State Committee of Defence'. His decorations are listed. They still include the Order of Suvorov.

Quite apart from the unavoidable matter of the *Encyclopaedia* other occasions began to occur in which something had to be said about the rehabilitated nations. 1957, for instance, was celebrated as the 400th Anniversary of the accession of Kabarda to Russia. (In other countries, as Mr. Kolarz says, the anniversary of their independence is celebrated, but for the nations of the U.S.S.R. it is the anniversary of their submission. In October 1957, the Karachai had to go through the same celebrations.) This event was celebrated with considerable pomp. One of the ceremonies was a meeting in the Kremlin, on June 20th, 1957, at which the main speech was made by R.S.F.S.R. First Vice-Premier Sapinov, who said that the Russian people 'has always been the reliable friend of the peoples of Kabarda and Balkaria'. This seemed to confirm that the official intention was to suppress, as far as possible, mention of some unpleasant facts.

In connection with the anniversary, *A History of Kabarda* edited by N. A. Smirnov was published by the Academy of Sciences of the U.S.S.R. (passed for the Press on May 6th, 1957). There has been no recent history of the deported nations themselves, and this work on the Kabardines might be expected to give us more information both as to the facts and as to the attitude of the Soviet authorities than any similar work. For the Kabardines had, while remaining in good odour themselves, been previously in administrative relations with the deported Balkars.

The book's references to the Balkars are comparatively few. It does indeed mention the 'historical relations' between Kabarda and Balkaria, and speaks of how the Kabardines and Balkars living in the mountains had been connected by the movements of flocks of each to the area of the other during the relevant seasons.

Though the only political figure with a photograph in the book is Stalin, the general tone is on the whole very much more objective than those of the Stalin period, and it takes the present line that although the resistance movements against the Tsarist annexation were reactionary, they nevertheless were of a national resistance character.

This objectivity becomes less and less noticeable as we reach the time of the 1917 revolution, and more particularly in the years after that event. We are, however, told certain once

N

suppressed facts: that in January 1921 a Decree of the All-Russian Central Executive Committee set up the Mountain A.S.S.R., including 'Kabarda, Balkaria, Ossetia, Chechnia, Ingushetia', etc. It is admitted that 'Kulak banditism' resulted as late as 1921 in a state of war being declared in Kabarda.

The later administrative history of the territory is correctly described, Balkars and all: In September 1921, the setting up of a Kabardine autonomous province, in 1922 the inclusion of Balkaria in the province, and its renaming as Kabardine-Balkar Autonomous Province, and the setting up in 1937 of a Kabardine-Balkar A.S.S.R. On several occasions the whole territory is referred to, even though the Balkars are not much treated separately. For instance 'the nations' of Kabardino-Balkaria, are stated to have benefited from a complete cultural revolution in the thirties. It is stated that on September 12th, 1937, in the elections the Supreme Soviet of the U.S.S.R., 'in the whole Republic 98·6 of the electors took part in the voting. Of this number 99·7 voted for the candidate of the bloc of Communists and non-party men in the Supreme Soviet, and 99·5 for the Soviet of nationalities'. That is, the Balkars, who were to be shown as mass traitors, were virtually unanimous in the election. Similar (indeed better) results were obtained in the elections for the Supreme Soviet of the Republic in June 1938 — 99·9 of the electors voted, and of these 99·95 voted for the Party list.

The most interesting part of the history of the territory would have been an account of what precisely caused the trouble with the Balkars in the war, followed by the circumstances of their deportation and of their return, together with an estimate of their present numbers. Although sixty-two pages deal with the period in question, these facts do not emerge. But still, there are signs of unsatisfactory co-operation.

To weaken the resistance of the Caucasian nations Fascist propaganda spread rumours about special peaceful connections between Fascist Germany and the mountaineers, made efforts to divide the Russians and the mountaineers, and sowed national dissension.

The Germans, who occupied the territory for from two to five months, are stated to have been strongly resisted. But again, in October 1942 the Provincial Committee of the Party

> uncovered errors and inadequacies in the work of the provincial and regional Party organizations, including the leadership of the partisan movement in the regions of the republic occupied by the enemy, which expressed themselves in inadequate struggle against bourgeois nationalist elements, in the service of the Hitlerite occupiers.

The Germans are said to have brought back princes, kulaks and others driven out by the revolution and some attempt is made to imply that these were the main offenders. Among the crimes of the Germans and 'their bourgeois nationalist lackeys' the fact that 'they annihilated the kolkhozes and sovkhozes' is prominently stated. Much is made of the partisan movement, but most of its named members appear to be Russians, and its 'faults' included the fact that it did not organize bases in the rear of the enemy, but only infiltrated from time to time from behind the Soviet Army's lines.

By January 1943 the Republic had been entirely liberated, and a great deal of detail is given about economic and other measures. Here again the working people 'of the whole Republic actively took part'. And they 'voluntarily' subscribed to loans and to special levies for equipping forces. Politically it is said that 'the Central Committee of the Party approved the work of the Provincial Committee', but again mentioned certain 'errors and insufficiencies'.

> The Central Committee considered that although the bourgeois nationalist elements had been struck a blow in the first period after the driving out of the German Fascist occupiers, there were still in the Republic facts showing bourgeois nationalist ideology, and also the revival of private property moods

and other lesser troubles. Finally the deportation of the Balkars is described and condemned as follows:

> In 1944 the Kabardine-Balkar A.S.S.R. was changed into the Kabardine A.S.S.R. in connection with the fact that at the end of 1943 and beginning of 1944 all the Balkars were deported

without reason from the territory of the Republic. This repressive measure, carried out in connection with the whole people, constituted a crude breach of socialist legality and of Leninist principles of national policy.

In 1945 the twenty-fifth anniversary of Kabardine autonomy was celebrated, and thereafter several chapters deal with economic and cultural progress. In 1954 and 1955, it is added, 99 per cent of the electors voted for the Party list in the national and local elections. Finally,

> The Central Committee of the Communist Party and the Government of the U.S.S.R., in connection with the decisions of the Twentieth Congress of the C.P.S.U., put into effect measures to rehabilitate the Balkar nation and the correction of the injustices carried out in connection with it. In February 1957, the session of the Supreme Soviet confirmed a decree of the Presidium of the Supreme Soviet of the U.S.S.R. on the restoration of the national autonomy of the Balkar nation, and the renaming of the Kabardine A.S.S.R. the Kabardine-Balkar A.S.S.R. Practical measures for the reconstruction of the Republic were made the responsibility of the Council of Ministers of the K.B. A.S.S.R., together with representatives of the Balkar nation. The Kabardine nation, for many years in comradeship and brotherhood with the Balkar people, heartily approved this just decision.

A few other recent publications, mainly cultural, deal with the rehabilitated nations, and in a curious manner. For example, *The Musical Culture of the Autonomous Republics of the R.S.F.S.R.*, edited by G. I. Litinsky (Moscow, 1957), has sections on the Kabardine-Balkar and Chechen-Ingush A.S.S.R.s. In both cases a considerable amount of historical background is given, but without any reference to the deportation. The Balkars, like the Kabardines, are said to have been allowed to remain in economic and cultural backwardness by Tsarist Russia;

> Soviet Kabardino-Balkaria shows itself in present times as a flourishing area, where with every year socialist industry and village economy equipped with advanced technique, grows stronger . . . . A Kabardine-Balkar culture, socialist in content and national in form thrives and develops.

The Balkars are described as 'tenacious, bold, rough and hardworking', as a result of their mountain life. Their attachment to the Soviet state, in the past as well as now, is demonstrated by the fact that 'the events connected with the Great October Revolution found a most convincing echo in the creations of the Balkar people'. As an example songs are given (dated 1940, 1941, 1957) in praise of Kirov, of the Party and Komsomol, and of Lenin. The last is quoted: 'Lenin gave us the Party, and the Party brought the poor folk to freedom and happiness.' It is also noted that much of Balkar popular creation is concerned with

Kolkhoz songs and songs of the new life. The old customs are disappearing with the centuries-old prejudices. The new, healthy life is supplanting outworn connections.

Incidentally the poet Kazim Mechaes, described as 'the founder of Balkar literature', is mentioned as dying in 1945, but where and how is not stated.

The article (by N. Rechmensky) on the Chechen-Ingush A.S.S.R.'s music is the only one with which there are no photographs of artistic activities (those of the Kabardine-Balkar A.S.S.R. appear to be all of Kabardines). A description of the agrarian and other riches of the republic is followed by a historical sketch beginning, 'The history of the Chechens and Ingushi, these freedom-loving and warrior peoples, has been little studied and still awaits its researchers.' It mentions the legendary origins, contact with Russia, Tsarist Conquest, popular movements under Mansur, Shamil and others, to the time when the Revolution ended the 'persecutions and oppressions which the Chechens and Ingushi suffered at the hand of the colonizers'. The Revolution brought 'complete liberation from centuries of slavery'. Both peoples fought heroically against the White Guards in the Civil War. Of their history since 1917 only this is said:

There was much change in the life and existence of the Chechens and Ingushi after the victory of October. Serious attention was paid to questions of culture and the education of the people. Art gained unlimited opportunities for development.

Some of the resulting songs are quoted. For instance, there is one song of 'Ingush maidens' which runs as follows:

> The Tsar-enemy kept the workers in darkness.
> But they won justice in heroic struggle.
> Soviet people, Ingushi, know
> How the workers gained your rights.
> We will construct a new life,
> We will strengthen the kolkhozes.
> We will fulfil the five-year plan in three years.

Songs to Lenin are also quoted, and a longer Chechen song about the October Revolution, as a result of which,

> We abolished the old laws,
> A happy youth grows in our land . . . .
> The Communist Party goes from victory to victory,
> It increases the sowing of the Kolkhoz fields,
> It defeats the enemy, standing in the way,
> It uproots the concealed traitor.

The Chechens and Ingushi finally are again said to be 'constructing their own culture, socialist in content and national in form, in the fraternal family of the peoples of the soviet socialist republics'. And that is all.

This sort of treatment of the rehabilitated nations is more or less typical of what is now being given in Soviet publications. It seems particularly inadequate and unconvincing. In effect, the same is being said about the Chechens or the Balkars now as used to appear in Soviet propaganda in the period before the war. Their cultural and political situation is represented as splendid and their devotion to the Soviet regime as immense. This was evidently untrue before the war, and it would strain anyone's credulity to imagine that loyalty and contentment have increased as a result of the experiences of the past fifteen years. Moreover, the simple hushing up of those injustices is grotesque: no one would expect the Soviet rulers, especially in their present mood, to dwell on the deportations much, but no good can come of insulting the intelligence of readers by such *suppressio veri*, combined with the obvious *suggestio falsi* implied by the remarks actually made about the peoples concerned. In general, such an attitude to truth, and to objective history (of which these are by no means the only examples), is bound to make all observers uneasy. It is obviously dangerous for all of us to have a great state ruled by men for whom a party decision displaces a fact.

Chapter 14

THE MEANING OF THESE EVENTS

————◆◇◆————

Part of this book simply gives the early historical background of the nations deported. The remainder deals
with their experience under Soviet rule and with the
Soviet theory of how nationalities should be treated. With a
few exceptions, which have been indicated, the material for
this part is based entirely on Soviet official documents. Nor are
the exceptions essential to the argument: they merely illustrate
and develop certain points.

It is perfectly true that my method of approach to Soviet
documents in this sphere might be called selective. A round-up
of everything that has been printed in the Soviet Union
relevant to the minority question would probably show that
99 per cent of it consisted of accounts of progress and assertions
of general contentment. Is it then unfair to have concentrated
largely on the 1 per cent which does not?

The answer should be obvious enough and the only reason
why it seems worth raising the issue at all is that books do
appear which take the other view. There is, for instance, *The
Nationalities Problem and Soviet Administration*, edited by Dr.
Schlesinger (Routledge & Kegan Paul, 1956) — an anthology
of meaningless Soviet documents. The last part of this book
purports to give the type of Soviet evidence on which 'critical
study of the existing books' should be based. It produces for
this purpose three anodyne examples of official nonsense. And
it disagrees with Mr. Walter Kolarz's books on Soviet nationality policy as being from the point of view of 'the bourgeois
nationalists'!

But this sort of quasi-objective academicism is beside the point. If a thousand documents say that the minor nationalities of the U.S.S.R. enjoy all the autonomy they wish and one document admits that most of those who had the opportunity were involved in mass efforts to overthrow the Soviet regime, then that one document refutes the 999 others and they are no longer worth studying except as examples of official propaganda. (In much the same way ninety-nine letters protesting innocence are unable to refute one finger-print on the revolver.) It is true that certain of these documents appear more objective than others in that they give figures indicating prosperity. This is not a book in which I can discuss the question of Soviet statistics at any length, but at least one can say that anyone who accepts them as they stand is probably inclined to be overly impressed by the mere fact that they are official. After all, a regime which falsifies the evidence in a show trial, as has been admitted, is quite capable of making up a set of figures. And previous chapters of this book have given examples of covert and overt falsification which may be sufficient to prove this point.

The relevance of the events in the North Caucasus and the Crimea to Soviet national policy as a whole seems clear. Of the non-Russian nationalities of the Soviet Union, the Germans reached or very closely approached the territories of two groups:

(1) the Esthonians, Latvians, Lithuanians, Byelorussians and Ukrainians — the European and mainly Slav population of the border area, each of them forming an allegedly sovereign union republic and none numbering less than a million,

and

(2) the small nations of Asian origin in the southern fringe of the Slav lands: the Crimean Tatars, the Kalmyks, the Circassians (Cherkess and Adygei), the Karachai, the Balkars, the Kabardines, the Ossetians, the Chechens and the Ingushi. These small nations may be taken as a reasonably representative cross-section of the general Asian population of the U.S.S.R. — mostly Mohammedan,

though the Kalmyks are Buddhist. (The Ossetians are indeed more Christianized and Russianized than is largely typical.)

It will be seen that of the second group it was felt that six out of ten had proved not simply disloyal, but disloyal to the extent of mass treachery. There seems no reason to regard this as exceptional, and it may be taken as a plebiscite which would have given similar results if it had been held among any other of the U.S.S.R.'s minority groups. As to the largely European peoples in the first group, evidence of their opposition to Soviet rule and the fact that they took advantage of the German invasion to demonstrate it (though not necessarily in co-operation with the Germans — the Ukrainian 'Benderovtsy' seem to have fought both sides) is far greater than in the case of the Caucasian peoples. Deportation on an enormous scale took place among them, particularly in the Western Ukraine and in the Baltic States. Serov's next post, following on his assignment in the Crimea in June 1944, was to perform similar acts in Lithuania. It appears that at least a million people were deported from the three Baltic states — a large number, though not of course the same as the attack in the Caucasus on entire nations. Yet practical, theoretical and propaganda difficulties rather than any lack of ill-will seem to have been all that stood in the way of the complete dispersion of these nations too. Khrushchev states in his Secret Speech that the Ukrainians avoided meeting this fate only because there were too many of them and there was no place to which to deport them. Otherwise Stalin would have deported them also (a statement greeted with 'laughter and animation in the hall').

Khrushchev states that blaming whole nations is contrary to Lenin's principles. If we accept this as self-evident, it must have been apparent to Khrushchev at the time of the deporta-tions, though he does not claim that he made any protest. What is more to the point is that it must have been as apparent in 1953 after Stalin's death as it was three years later. Yet no action was taken to relieve this injustice until the later date. It can hardly be argued that it was necessary for the leaders to be gradual in reversing Stalin's 'errors'. For they carried out a major reversal almost immediately after his death. This was the repudiation of the alleged Doctors' Plot. This imaginary conspiracy was, according to Khrushchev, concocted by Stalin with the design of purging the top leaders of the Party. In fact, when it came to injustice directed against themselves they were quick enough to act. Injustice affecting over a million ordinary people does not seem to have struck them as in need of nearly such urgent attention.

Responsibility for the deportations rests in the first place with Stalin. Next we may rank those members of the Politbureau who voted for his proposal, either because they approved it, or because they preferred their own skins to those of a million other human beings. Beria, executed in 1953, may be presumed to have had some executive responsibility, both as Politbureau delegate in the Caucasian region earlier (during military operations there), and as head of the police ministries involved. Suslov, who was Party Secretary in Stavropol at the relevant times, can probably be taken as concerned, at a lower level, in the recommendation and organization of at least the Karachai affair. Those immediately in charge were Ivan Serov, until lately head of the K.G.B., and still in a position of trust, and his subordinates Gvishiani and Goglidze.

Goglidze was tried with Beria and shot in December 1953 and Gvishiani is also believed to have been shot as a Beria supporter, though without any announcement being made. Goglidze, who was made Colonel-General in 1945 with other leading policemen, had been a candidate member of the Central Committee of the Party since 1939. He was accused, with the others on trial, of a large number of crimes including acting as 'agents of international imperialism'. A number of inhuman persecutions were also alleged against him and the others, but these were all persecutions directed against important members of the Communist Party, and no reference was made to there having been anything wrong with his actions in the Northern Caucasus. Kobulov, another of those shot with Beria, has been reported as concerned in the Crimean deportation. Another police official reported to have had a hand in the deportations, Kruglov, was Minister of the Interior from the fall of Beria until early in 1956, but has since sunk into obscurity.

Serov, on the other hand, has not been tried, or censured, or even deprived of his ill-earned Order of Suvorov. Dr. Lydia Timashuk, an instigator of the Doctors' Plot frame-up, was strongly condemned afterwards, and the Order of Lenin she had been awarded for her vigilance was withdrawn. The man who actually carried out Stalin's orders in that case, Deputy Minister of State Security Ryumin, was shot for it. The deportations are condemned as another of Stalin's crimes. But this time his chief agent receives no blame.

The Soviet Union seems by its attitude at the Nuremberg War Crimes Trial to have committed itself to a refusal to accept as a defence for criminal acts that they were committed under orders. (Indeed Khrushchev himself rejects that defence in the case of another police official, Rodos — whose crime, however, was the maltreatment of leading Communists.) It seems reasonable to ask why Serov and others are not proceeded against. The signature by the Soviet Union of the United Nations Genocide Convention binds its government to prevent *and punish* it. It would seem that in principle there is a *prima facie* case for United Nations inquiry about that government's fulfilment of its obligations.

It may be relevant that, in his Secret Speech, Khrushchev concludes his catalogue of Stalin's crimes, including these deportations by saying:

> This question is complicated by the fact that all this which we have just discussed was done during Stalin's life under his leadership and with his concurrence; here Stalin was convinced that this was necessary for the defence of the interests of the working classes against the plotting of enemies and against the attack of the imperialist camp.
>
> He saw this from the position of the interest of the working class, of the interest of the labouring people, of the interest of the victory of socialism and communism. We cannot say that these were the deeds of a giddy despot. He considered that this should be done in the interest of the party, of the working masses, in the

name of the defence of the revolution's gains. In this lies the whole tragedy!

This casts some sinister light on the whole matter. For it presents such things as these deportations as acts, judged after some years of consideration by his successors to be erroneous, indeed, but yet capable of being committed in good faith by an honest Communist: mistakes due to misjudgment rather than tyranny.

The extent to which any feeling for the realities of nationalism has simply disappeared from the minds of the leading figures in the U.S.S.R. may be seen from another passage in Khrushchev's Secret Speech. In it he condemns Stalin for framing up certain party leaders in Georgia in the 'Mingrelian case'. These men had allegedly formed a nationalist organization to detach Georgia from the U.S.S.R. Khrushchev asks rhetorically if it were possible that nationalist tendencies had grown so great that there was any real danger of this. His answer is instructive:

This is, of course, nonsense. It is impossible to imagine how such assumptions could enter anyone's mind. Everyone knows how Georgia has developed economically and culturally under Soviet rule.

Industrial production of the Georgian Republic is 27 times greater than it was before the Revolution. Many new industries have arisen in Georgia which did not exist there before the Revolution: iron smelting, an oil industry, a machine-construction industry, etc. Illiteracy has long since been liquidated, which, in pre-Revolutionary Georgia, included 78 per cent of the population.

Could the Georgians, comparing the situation in their republic with the hard situation of the working masses in Turkey, be aspiring to join Turkey? In 1955, Georgia produced 9 times as much electrical energy per person as Turkey. According to the available 1950 census, 65 per cent of Turkey's total population are illiterate, and, of the women, 80 per cent are illiterate. Georgia has 19 institutions of higher learning which have about 39,000 students; this is 8 times more than in Turkey (for each 1,000 inhabitants). The prosperity of the working people has grown tremendously in Georgia under Soviet rule.

It is clear that, as the economy and culture develop, and as the socialist consciousness of the working masses in Georgia grows, the source from which bourgeois nationalism draws its strength evaporates.

It will be seen that on Khrushchev's view nationalism cannot exist in Georgia because its industry is more highly developed than other countries in the Middle East. At its very best this is simply a crude form of paternalism.

Even if we allow the minor premise that the Georgian masses are economically satisfied (and there is considerable reason to doubt this) the major premise is an astonishing piece of naïveté. National feeling has never been even in the slightest degree satisfied with foreign rule simply because it brings prosperity. To anyone who is not politically illiterate dozens of refutations will occur at once.

Moreover the way in which Khrushchev argues is an abdication of political realism. It may or may not be true that any particular feeling exists anywhere: but to rule it out as *a priori* impossible on scholastic grounds means that the authorities no longer feel themselves obliged to examine evidence outside their own documents. (The evidence refuting Khrushchev's view was in fact provided only a month after it was put forward, in the Tbilisi riots of March 1956.) But this sort of thinking is only too typical of the whole Soviet outlook. (It is similar to the view often met with that there can be no strikes in a Communist country because the state is a workers' state and therefore the workers would have no interest in striking against it, or to the even more disquieting notion that since a Socialist state is by definition incapable of aggression, no military action it takes, of any sort whatever, can be called aggressive.)

Where there is oppression ordered from outside and carried out largely by foreigners, the inevitable resistance will take national form — even though the original oppressive measures have no specific national character. This proposition, which has been largely forgotten by the Soviet leaders, seems to be the key to the enormous strength of national feeling in the Soviet bloc. The case of Hungary was a particularly striking demonstration of the theme.

Certainly the Soviet Government has made partial amends

for the deportation decisions taken by Stalin. And as we have seen, Khrushchev condemned Stalin's action in the matter as contrary to Leninist principles.

What this means is not so certain. Lenin certainly laid down as a general principle that nations should be treated on a basis of equality. But, as was shown in Chapter 8, he makes it clear that in practice the interests of a given nation may be contrary to those of the world revolution, and that in that case its national interests may, and in fact must, be suppressed.

If the aspirations of a nation clash with those of the world revolution (incarnate in the government of the Soviet Union), perhaps to the extent of looking towards independence, the case against it would be established. If such a nation were in a strategic area, the interests of the Soviet Union might well require its deportation. And in fact, in rather a different context, Khrushchev opposed turning the Crimea into a Jewish settlement area on the grounds that *that* nation's habitation of the area would turn it into a 'place d'armes' against the Soviet Union. And the fact that the Crimea was the only truly strategic area involved in the deportations, and that it is one of the two in which Khrushchev has *not* felt it necessary to permit the re-establishment of the national rights might be taken to imply that he differs from Stalin not in principle but simply in holding a less strict interpretation of what areas are strategically sensitive. If this is so, it is an opinion depending on military factors which might change, and on military opinions which might vary. In that case there can be no guarantee that the stricter view might not again prevail in Soviet government circles, and further trouble ensue for unsatisfactory nations.

For, in any case, while Khrushchev condemns the policy pursued by Stalin in the matter, he nowhere condemns in any way the structure of Soviet rule which makes such a decision possible. That the governing councils of the Soviet Union sitting at the Kremlin actually decided to deport these nations is indeed reprehensible, as Khrushchev says. But it is equally reprehensible that they should be *in a position to do so at all*. It is hard to follow how it can be maintained that the nations of the U.S.S.R. have any rights or powers, when these are admittedly abolished or restored by simple fiat from Moscow. Now, as before, the national minorities of the U.S.S.R. depend, even for their very existence, upon policy decisions in which they have no say.

It seems probable that the main reason for the announcement of the repatriation of the deported peoples has been the pressure of opinion in Free Asia. Some of the facts had become fairly widely known, and in the present period when Asian good-will is important in Soviet foreign policy, a balance of advantage may be thought to have lain in the course now taken. That pressure of world opinion may, in such circumstances, have some effect in the U.S.S.R. is a very welcome state of affairs, and the fact that some measure of relief has thus been afforded to the decimated populations is most encouraging. It cannot be concealed, however, that attention to the susceptibilities of Asians not under Soviet rule is one thing and that any genuine feeling about the rights of the nations already within the Soviet Union is another. And the only too obvious implication is that if ever *all* the Asian populations came within the Communist belt, these pressures would no longer exist and there would be no reason to expect any concessions from Moscow.

Even as it is, such pressures, and whatever other motives the Soviet leaders may have for the changes of policy, are no substitute for real guarantees of the rights of the smaller nations of the Soviet Union. 'The Soviet Government giveth and the Soviet Government taketh away. Blessed be the Soviet Government' is not a formula that is likely to be subscribed to with any enthusiasm by local patriots.

Even on the personality level, and even if we accept Khrushchev's thesis and blame the whole business on Stalin, no constitutional changes have taken place in the U.S.S.R. to prevent the emergence of another Stalin. Nor have the present rulers of the Soviet Union showed themselves to differ in principle on questions of national rights, as was shown in

Hungary in November 1956. Their view of policy may tend to make them less ready to give such obvious affronts to national aspirations as Stalin did in the deportations. But this is only a comparative matter and when Soviet interest appeared to be affected in an important way in Budapest, they were ready enough to act.

In any case, the fate of the subject nations continues to depend solely on decisions taken in Moscow. The great lesson of the actions taken in 1941 to 1944 and described in these pages is simply that no sanction exists to modify those decisions, even when they are to the effect that a nation's existence shall cease.

In any case, 'bourgeois nationalism' remains the enemy. Attacks on it have not ceased even in the most relaxed periods. And a new campaign was launched in the first months of 1958, when the Communist Parties of the non-Russian republics of the U.S.S.R. held their biennial Congresses. All the Party Secretaries appealed for vigilance against ideologies smuggled in by 'the enemy'. Much of the attack was directed against nationalism. In all the peripheral republics particular attention was paid to 'unhealthy moods' among students and intellectuals. In Tadzhikistan Uldzhabaev and other Party speakers went to the length of attacking the spreaders of 'hostile rumours' and even the circulation of 'slanderous and anonymous documents'. Mustafaev, the First Secretary in Azerbaijan said:

> It is no secret that propaganda hostile to us often tries to play on the national feelings of certain people. We must, therefore, be exceptionally vigilant. Every attempt of hostile elements to undermine the friendship of Soviet peoples, to sow in our midst the poisonous seed of nationalism and chauvinism must be cut short in a most merciless manner.

o

Chapter 15

SOME CONCLUSIONS

———————◄◦◦◦►———————

One important thing that seems to be shown by these rehabilitations is that the Soviet government, having embarked on a particularly energetic campaign to seek popularity abroad, and in particular in the Asian countries, can no longer remain as impervious to foreign public opinion as in Stalin's time. The approaches and inquiries made by Asian governments in the case of some of these peoples and the fair (though entirely inadequate) publicity the deportations belatedly began to receive in Asia and elsewhere in recent years, were considerable drags on the effectiveness of the Soviet publicity machine in the countries concerned. It may be, as we have said, that such considerations only lead to the correction of abuses after a careful consideration of the balance of advantages. If so, the case of the Crimean Tatars has evidently not been thought sufficient to make the advantages abroad of their rehabilitation compensate for the disadvantage of having them in the Crimea. Yet, even so, the fact that foreign opinion now has an effect of any sort on the internal practices of the Soviet Union is a great improvement on the position in Stalin's time. And even in those cases where it may seem unlikely that the Soviet Government would be willing to make the necessary political sacrifices, it seems well worth-while for foreign opinion to speak out. We need no longer feel that the voice of protest is *necessarily* ineffective. And this should encourage anyone concerned with national oppression or individual suffering to continue to raise the relevant matters on all suitable occasions.

On the particular issue, if we accept the view that foreign

opinion was one of the factors which produced the rehabilitation, there was plainly a period when it was felt that it could be ignored. And the reason seems plain: there was little sign of much concern, or even much knowledge, about the deportations. Far lesser measures of oppression elsewhere have raised enormous excitement and resentment. The absence of almost any news of the lost nations of Russia, apart from the fact of their deportation, contrasted with the continual stream of information from (say) Cyprus. It was in a way a situation similar to that which existed in Western Europe in the week in which Willi Göttling was shot without trial in East Berlin and the Rosenbergs were executed in America. People when pressed would admit that reason and duty required them to be as concerned and excited about Göttling as about the Rosenbergs, or more so. But reason and duty are not sufficient to provoke the emotions of interest or sympathy. We require also the personal touch, the details of personal or national life, of personal or national struggle, which can enable us to identify ourselves to some extent with the victims. As far as this goes the Iron Curtain paid the Soviet authorities.

This being the case, the least that any conscientious citizen of free Europe or free Asia might do was as far as he could to correct his own emotions and to see that the facts become as widely known and as much understood as possible. It was probably due at least in part to the devoted efforts of a few members of these nations who had escaped, and a few publicists and political figures in India, Burma and elsewhere, that most, though not all, of these nations were rehabilitated after thirteen years in exile. A clear understanding of Soviet national policy remains the duty of all who concern themselves with political realities.

It may be that there are other minor hindrances to an understanding of Russian colonialism. It has often been pointed out that the Soviet Union, consisting of contiguous territories, looks a more natural political unit than do the French or British empires, and that imperialism by land can be a more gradual and less obvious process than imperialism by sea. After

O2

a few generations it becomes difficult to remember that the Caucasus is not part of Russia, while no one would ever think that Kenya was part of Great Britain. But, of course, the Russian conquest of the Caucasus and Central Asia was carried on at the same time as the British conquests in India and Africa. The peoples were subjugated and in a more complete fashion. The British have commenced a genuine withdrawal. The Russians performed a token withdrawal in the form of the granting of alleged autonomies, but in reality strengthened their grip.

In any case, it is to be hoped that as far as possible attention can be directed in future as much to the greater but more concealed abuses of the Communist empires as to the lesser, but more publicized ones of the West. Without being Utopian, even a slight improvement might not only contribute to preventing suffering in the Soviet bloc, but also help to create a world public opinion better informed about important facts, and hence more realistic in general.

The most obvious and the most important conclusion that one is bound to come to is, of course, that the rulers of the Soviet Union are in principle quite ruthless (though their rigour may be moderated by considerations of political advantage) and that this ruthlessness may be directed against entire nations as much as against individuals. There is no need to labour this point, which will in any case hardly be a new one to anyone after the events in Hungary.

It seems more important to consider the long-term political significance of the actions described in this book. What seems to emerge is that the authorities in Moscow are committed to complete centralism as far as actual power and policies are concerned. The changes in attitude to the minority nations can only be seen as tactical ones, within those limitations. Sometimes more, sometimes less, concession is made to local feeling in an effort to secure as far as possible the acceptance of inessential concessions to national feeling as a substitute for the essential.

Yet here, as in other spheres, Soviet authorities find themselves caught in a contradiction. To take a single instance: the reviling of local national heroes like Shamil and the insistence on obeisance to all things Russian produces resentment. On the other hand admitting that Shamil was a heroic figure and allowing this to be taught in the local schools encourages national sentiment, and in a form which can hardly fail to be anti-Russian. The present compromise on this particular issue, whereby both sides are right, is a forced and unreal one and is likely to make the worst of both worlds.

In almost all spheres, indeed, the choice that seems to present itself to the Communist rulers is between oppression and relaxation. The experience of the past few years has shown that repression produces troubles which can apparently only be coped with by relaxation, but that relaxation then produces troubles which require repression. This is an old problem in autocracies and one which has never been satisfactorily solved.

As we have said, it seems that the influence of the non-Communist peoples is a factor, even if not a major one, even in Soviet internal affairs, and it is to be hoped that the humanitarian appeals of the uncommitted states which seem to have had their effect in this case, will be continued. But we may also consider the larger question of the type of policy to be pursued by the strong non-Communist powers whose existence is what now prevents the expansion of the Communist system over the whole world by force — and, following on that, the removal of most restraints on the Communist treatment of the smaller nations. At its lowest these national troubles in the U.S.S.R. indicate a weakness and at the level simply of cold war may be taken advantage of by opponents of Soviet expansion in the same way as the Soviet government does with comparable matters in the non-Communist world. But if we think more of the long-term aims of peace, the end of national and other oppressions, and a co-operative world, the criteria are rather different. Presumably it is in the interests of the non-Communist states to do whatever is possible to secure that the Soviet bloc progresses to a point at which its rulers are a threat neither to the outside world nor to their own populations. This does not imply that the government or governments should cease to be Communist or atheist or anything else — still less that the social structure requires revolutionary change. What it does mean is that the siege economy and polity which has prevailed for so many years must give way to government by consent, that the unnatural strains and stresses of a state constructed as the instrument of one-man rule against all the natural tendencies of society should alter to at least that extent.

What the West might do to improve matters seems to be two-fold. First, Western defensive arrangements must be such that no possible temptation to any irresponsible ruler in the Kremlin to aggression can exist. But secondly the West should continually make clear the circumstances in which a genuine peace could be found. No sort of threats or ultimata are needed: simply the continual pointing out of the escape-route from the contradictions and dangers of Soviet society.

It is true that a closed ideology dominates the Moscow government. Yet ideology does not exist in a vacuum. And we have seen in Yugoslavia how it is capable of evolving under the pressure of events. The pressures in Russia are exerted both by the strains in Soviet society, including the national question, and by the Western defences which prevent, or should prevent foreign adventures. The way out of this corral may not yet be visible to the short-sighted creatures trapped in it. But every Western speech and note could help by drawing attention to its existence.

In any case, whatever view may be taken of these matters of high policy, it is hoped that this book will contribute to the reader's insight into the whole Soviet way of thinking and of acting. Enormously important though the national question is in itself, the principles applied in it may also be regarded as typical of what is done and thought over the entire range of Communist political, social and cultural action.

APPENDIX I

RECONSTRUCTED CHRONOLOGY

28th Aug.	1941	Decree on the deportation of the Volga Germans.
7th Sept.	1941	Decree on the partition of the former Volga German Republic.
February	1943	Decision taken to deport certain nations.
Oct.-Nov.	1943	Deportation of the Karachai.
December	1943	Deportation of the Kalmyks.
27th Dec.	1943	Decree on the deportation of the Kalmyks and setting up of the Astrakhan Province.
21st Feb.	1944	Deportation of the Chechens and Ingushi.
7th Mar.	1944	Decree on the deportation of the Chechens and Ingushi.
9th Mar.	1944	Award of Order of Suvorov 1st Class to Serov.
22nd Mar.	1944	Setting up of the Grozny Province.
Mar.-Apr.	1944	Deportation of the Balkars.
June	1944	Deportation of the Crimean Tatars.
30th June	1944	Decree transforming the Crimean Republic into the Crimean Province.
26th June	1946	Publication of decree on the deportation of the Chechens, Ingushi and Crimean Tatars.
10th Feb.	1948	Central Committee pronouncement on music, attacking the Chechens and Ingushi.
May	1950	Denunciation of Shamil.
19th Feb.	1954	Decree transferring the Crimea from the R.S.F.S.R. to the Ukraine.
14th Mar.	1955	Decree transferring Karachai territory from Georgia to the R.S.F.S.R.

17th May	1955	First mention of Chechens in exile.
January	1956	First attempts to rehabilitate Shamil.
24-25 Feb.	1956	Khrushchev's Secret Speech.
9th Jan.	1957	Decrees of the Presidium of the Supreme Soviet on restoring the national autonomy of the Balkars, Chechens, Ingushi, Kalmyks and Karachai.
11th Jan.	1957	Decree of the Presidium of the Supreme Soviet on transfer of Chechen territory from Georgia to the R.S.F.S.R.
11th Feb.	1957	Gorkin's speech to the Supreme Soviet.
11th Feb.	1957	Law of the Supreme Soviet confirming decrees of January 9th and January 11th. Decree of the Supreme Soviet making the necessary constitutional changes.
March	1957	Official repudiation of rehabilitators of Shamil and imposition of a moderate Stalinist view.
29th July	1958	Decree transforming the Kalmyk Autonomous Province into the Kalmyk A.S.S.R.
September	1958	Publication of supplementary Volume 51 of the *Large Soviet Encyclopaedia*.
end of	1958	Prospective date for the completion of the return of the Kalmyks, Karachai and Balkars.
end of	1960	Prospective date for the completion of the return of the Chechens and Ingushi.

APPENDIX II

THE UNITED NATIONS GENOCIDE CONVENTION

A 'Convention on the Prevention and Punishment of the Crime of Genocide' was adopted by the United Nations General Assembly on December 9th, 1948. It came into effect in 1950 and was ratified by the U.S.S.R. in 1954. The substantive articles are as follows:

Article I
The contracting parties confirm that genocide, whether committed in time of peace or in time of war, is a crime under international law which they undertake to prevent and punish.

Article II
In the present Convention genocide means any of the following acts committed with intent to destroy, in whole or in part, a national, ethnical, racial or religious group, as such:
(a) Killing members of the group;
(b) Causing grievous bodily or mental harm to members of the group;
(c) Deliberately inflicting on the group conditions of life calculated to bring about its physical destruction in whole or in part;
(d) Imposing measures intended to prevent births within the group;
(e) Forcibly transferring children of the group to another group.

The second edition of the *Large Soviet Encyclopaedia* has an article on the subject in which it describes Genocide as 'an offshoot of decaying imperialism'.

PRINTED IN GREAT BRITAIN
BY ROBERT MACLEHOSE AND CO. LTD
THE UNIVERSITY PRESS, GLASGOW